MG Y TYPE SPORTS SALOON

NEIL CAIRNS

AMBERLEY

First published 2022

Amberley Publishing
The Hill, Stroud,
Gloucestershire, GL5 4EP

www.amberley-books.com

Copyright © Neil Cairns, 2022

The right of Neil Cairns to be identified as the Author
of this work has been asserted in accordance with the
Copyright, Designs and Patents Act 1988.

ISBN: 978 1 3981 0666 6 (print)
ISBN: 978 1 3981 0667 3 (ebook)

British Library Cataloguing in Publication Data.
A catalogue record for this book is available from the British Library.

Typeset in 10pt on 13pt Celeste.
Origination by Amberley Publishing.
Printed in the UK.

Contents

Preface

The MG Y Type is probably one of the prettiest and most elegant of the MG saloons. Its flowing lines are a real pleasure to the eye, and it hides its Morris Eight origins very well. It is also a model that when you tell someone you own an MG Y Type, you will often get a blank look returned, so be prepared to have to explain what one looks like. Also, at car shows people will ask if it is a Riley. For an MG model that was the first to be sold with independent front suspension, rack-and-pinion steering, the first to be available in left-hand-drive, whose suspension and steering was used until 1991 and whose chassis bore the TD and TF Midget sports cars, to be such a pleasure to drive as well as to accelerate and being the fastest in its class, it is a shame it is such a Cinderella. I am really pleased that Amberley Publishing have given me the chance to say my bit. I have been enjoying driving, maintaining, restoring and servicing my own 1952 MG YB for over twenty-five years now. I get asked what my car actually is even by modern MG owners. For my sins, I am also the 'technical advice chap' to the MG Car Club, Y Type Register and the MG Octagon Car Club. I also appear to be a bit of an MG engine expert and get queries about the XPAG from all over the world. The Y Type is also one of the rarer MGs of today.

Acknowledgements

There is no way any book like this can be written without recourse to the experiences and photos of other like-minded people. Many of them could probably write a book as well. Where I have used a photo not my own, there is the name of its contributor in the photo's caption. They are from Andrew Moreland, Alan Chick, Peter Veilvoye, Gerry Birkbeck, Ted Gardner, Brown and Gammons, and the British Motor Industry Heritage Trust. It must be remembered many photos used are just snapshots taken long before the digital camera, so some will be pin-sharp, but others will not. I had help in this task from many people; special mention should go to Peter Veilvoye, Lisa at BMIHT and Chris Callaghan. The MGCC Y Register approve of the book.

Introduction

The MG Y Type, as it is known today, is a 1930s car. It has one of the longest names of any MG car, the 'MG One and a Quarter Litre, Six-Light, Sports Saloon'. (Six-light refers to the side windows.) In 1939, it was originally to be called the MG Ten relating to its horsepower. Due to the Second World War it was shelved and introduced eight years later in 1947. It was one of a set of three luxurious saloon cars by MG. It was Cecil Kimber's dream to break into that market, having done extremely well in the sports car section. By 1939 there was already a medium saloon in the 14-hp VA and the big, impressive 18-hp SA that evolved into the WA. MG intended to put the new MG Ten alongside their little sports car the TB, the VA and WA on their 1940 London Motor Show stand, but world events scotched that idea. This pretty little sports saloon was a quite modern design that was born in the Morris office in Cowley, near Oxford. It was assembled at Abingdon and, like all other MGs, it used in-house corporate parts – bin components for ease of supply, interchangeability and low cost. It also hid some very innovating designs that were used by MG up until the MG RV8. One can stun MGB owners when asked to look under a Y Type, as very few realise both cars use the same steering and suspension. Sadly, there are no company records for the Y Type as these were lost or destroyed in the early 1960s in an office tidy up. Only a few pages of the despatch ledger records exist, and then only of the last few cars. MG used the alphabet to code its cars; the Y Series was followed by the Z Magnette in 1953, so they started with the A again in 1954 with the MGA. There are three models of the Y Types: the YA, YT and YB.

This is not a straightforward history of the car. It delves into the ancestry of the model and is liberally punctuated with twenty-five years' experience of running a Y, the good bits and bad bits, full of advice, hints and tips of keeping such an elderly car on the road safely.

1

The Birth of the Y

Every story has to have a beginning and in the case of the little 1939 MG 10 hp that grew into the 1947 MG Series Y Type sports saloon, we start with the Morris Eight Series E. Between the First and Second World Wars the huge Morris Motors Company was one of the – if not the – biggest car-making firms in the United Kingdom. It was wholly owned in Oxford by William Morris, who started out like so many other similar concerns, as a bicycle manufacturer. 'Manufacturer' is not really the correct word as, like most of the others of his time, proprietary parts were bought in from other firms and assembled, then given a company transfer and sold as such. Morris also dabbled in motorcycles for a very short time and again bought pre-made components and assembled them. This all led to William

The XPJM engine in a Morris Ten Series M – almost identical to a Y externally.

Morris starting up his own car manufacturing business, but not by making his own parts as Austin did; instead, he got others to make them for him, then gradually bought them out as he became their main – and often only – customer. Like Ford, Morris aimed for the mass-market of the middle and upper-middle classes. In those days cars were taxed on their 'horsepower' (hp) by a formula worked out for the treasury by the Royal Automobile Club (RAC). This annual tax was supposed to pay for the upkeep of the roads, but quickly found its way into the general tax pool for use in other government departments. Originally the horsepower tax was pretty accurate as it was based on the cylinder bore of the engine and ignored the stroke, just as in steam engine practice where the area of the piston gave the nominal power of the engine – hence nominal horsepower. The length or stroke of the piston was of little importance because a steam engine, like an electric motor, can give its full torque at zero rpm (revolutions per minute). So, the RAC used a similar method of deciding the power of an internal-combustion engine (ICE). This suited the Exchequer and so it was applied to cars up until 1945.

A system of power ratings was soon settled into by the manufacturers and there were classes of cars in the 8-hp, 10-hp, 12-hp, 14-hp, 18-hp, 20-hp, etc., ranges. (The Austin 7 was in fact an 8-hp car and was taxed as such.) Cecil Kimber, the man who founded the MG marque, had started to increase his company's range of cars in the 1930s. He had a 14-hp MG VA saloon, followed by a bigger 18-hp MG SA that evolved into the WA. These were based on the Wolseley range of cars that Morris made. Morris had bought up Wolseley when they went bust in 1935, mainly for their excellent engines, but also to stop Austin buying the same company – Austin started his career at Wolseley. Both Wolseley and MG used the mass-produced, in-house components of the Morris cars – a very logical and clever idea as it kept costs down but satisfied the markets. The Morris was a base model, the

The Morris Ten Series M Bakelite dashboard, originally intended for the MG Ten.

family car; the Wolseley was the upmarket version of the Morris, having its own bonnet and grill. In the case of MG, while the chassis and running gear was basically Morris much better-styled bodies by Kimber himself were fitted. By now Morris had bought up all his suppliers, so they were under his control.

William Morris rose to become Lord Nuffield and he personally owned Morris Motors, Wolseley Motors, MG (later Riley) and the individual companies he had bought up, such as Hoshkiss et Cie who were now the Morris Engines Branch. This wealth led him to become one of the – if not the – richest men in the world, which led to the tax man showing a great deal of interest. To get round this he sold all his companies to the Nuffield Group and this became a public limited company (PLC) with shares on the open market. As this was a big concern he took in a managing director to run the firm, one irascible Leonard Lord. Lord immediately took a grip on the very loosely run MG company, who had made a lot of sports cars in a multitude of models but made very little profit. Out went the specialist sections for racing and in came the diktat that all cars built by Nuffield would use common components. The MG enthusiasts know this as the beginning of the T Series sports cars where, except for the chassis and body, the whole set of running gear was that of the Morris Ten saloon car, complete with its modified side-valve (SV) engine to an overhead-valve (OHV) engine (MPJG, not a great success).

We come in here with those VA and SA/WA saloon cars where the chassis and running gear was that of the equivalent big Wolseley. Here, though, where the big Morris saloons had SV engines, the Wolseley and MG had the OHV equivalent. Lord had closed the MG design office at Abingdon and centred all Nuffield designs at the Morris main factory at Cowley, near Oxford, so the influence that MG could have on future MG models was reduced a great deal. Luckily, Kimber, a natural stylist, had a hand in the flowing lines of his big new saloons. This 'big saloon' market was one he was keen to break into as firms

The front beam axle on leaf springs of the Wolseley and Morris Ten, as seen on the original drawings of the MG Ten.

A MG YB and a Morris Ten Series M alongside each other – same body tub, different styling.

like SS Cars (later renamed Jaguar because of the Nazi connotations) were making similar and very popular models.

So, by the time 1938 arrived Kimber's big saloons were on the market with their excellent presence and flowing lines and ready to sell reasonably well. It was now time to get into the very, very popular 10-hp market. Morris had a 10-hp car for sale since the late 1920s, updating as other firms did year by year. By 1938 the Morris Ten Series M was a very up-to-date and modern car indeed, and only beaten by Vauxhall's 10-hp one. Vauxhall, since being taken over by General Motors (GM) of the USA, had left its rather staid big posh saloons behind and was heading to become one of the bigger UK manufacturers. Its 10-hp Wyvern was now a four-door family saloon with a chassisless monocoque body, OHV engine, synchromesh gearbox and independent from suspension by torsion bar. It was sold as a four-cylinder 10 hp and a six-cylinder 14 hp using the same car. Morris was not far behind with its 10-hp model, the Series M. It too was a monocoque and initially was to have rack-and-pinion steering with independent front suspension (IFS). The accountants by now had great sway in company decisions and the Series M left the factory with a cheaper front beam axle with leaf springs (called cart-sprung by enthusiasts) from its predecessor SV 10-hp model. It also kept the worm-and-peg steering box. It was this suspension and braking system that the TA MG Midget adopted, along originally with the slightly enlarged earlier Morris 10-hp OHV engine. The IFS designed by one Alexander Issigonis of later Mini fame was put on hold for the time being.

By the time the Morris Ten Series M arrived in 1938, that rather asthmatic OHV conversion of the original SV unit had been redesigned by Claud Bailey (of the later Jaguar twin-cam XK series engine designer) into a much more efficient unit with a shorter piston stroke of 1,140 cc. Its cylinder bore, though, made it a 10 hp for tax purposes. The factory dubbed it the 'Short-stroke Morris Ten Engine'. Prior to this the standard Morris engine's

A Morris rear door compared to a MG rear door.

stroke had been a massive 103 mm – the same as the much earlier Morris Bull Nose. The new shorter stroke was 89 mm, and this permitted the engine to rev much more freely. As a bored-out unit of 1,250 cc, it found its way into the MG TB sports car of 1939 – the very first XPAG. Inevitably, the Morris Ten Series M was also produced as a better-equipped Wolseley Ten/4.

The next monocoque (an integral chassis and body unit, today a normal way of building a car) Morris produced was a tidy little Morris Ten Series E. This replaced the rather upright Morris Eight, which had been a direct crib of the Ford Model Y (though its SV engine was a mirror image of the Ford product). It was the Morris Eight Series E body that would be used for Kimber's MG Ten. Here we see the results of a company existing of many smaller factions: the MG Ten and the Wolseley equivalent, while using the centre body section of the Morris, were mounted upon their own individual chassis. The Wolseley Ten/4 had a cruciform chassis, and the MG Ten a ladder chassis. This inevitably made these two cars rather heavy, defeating the object of a monocoque – we have a strong chassisless body mounted on a heavy steel chassis. It is not known why the Morris Ten Series M was not just fitted out with an MG radiator grill. The convolutions of the 10-hp and 8-hp range of Morris, MG and Wolseley cars can be confusing, so here is a simple 1938 list:

Morris Ten Series M
Monocoque body, leaf-sprung all round, worm-and-peg steering, 1,140-cc 10-hp OHV engine.

Wolseley Ten/4
Used the Morris Eight Series E body on a leaf-sprung cruciform chassis, worm-and-peg steering, 1,140-cc 10-hp OHV engine.

Morris Eight Series E
Monocoque body, 918-cc 8-hp SV engine, leaf sprung all round with worm-and-peg steering.

Wolseley Eight
Used Series E body leaf-sprung, worm-and-peg steering with a 918-cc OHV conversion of that 8-hp SV engine.

All had hydraulic drum brakes. It was from these Nuffield models that the MG Y Type arose.

The MG Ten

In 1937, MG were looking ahead to add a small saloon car to their range in the 10-hp bracket – very popular in those days. Virtually all the UK car companies had a model in this range, the 8-hp, 10-hp and 12-hp group being the bread and butter of the big manufacturers. MG were very lucky as they had the huge Nuffield organisation to pick and choose from. The MG Ten was built on a very stiff and strong ladder chassis with sides of 14 SWG mild steel, in a 5-in by 3-in box section using tubular cross members. It was reasonably light due to the thinner metal and upon it was mounted a stylistically modified Morris Eight Series E four-door, six-light body. The centre section of the Morris E's body tub was given running boards, a rear boot bustle and a longer nose. The original MG Ten had the suspension, steering and brakes of the E, as well as its rear axle. The MG was originally designed to be cart-sprung as all those other Nuffield cars were. Its boot lid had hidden hinges, so its

Note the MG's wing cuts into the door, making them non-interchangeable.

lower edge sank into the body when it was opened. As the car used the 8-hp body, it is seen today as a very small car and rather cramped for the big torsos of the twenty-first century. You might have to dissuade some of your bigger friends from cadging a lift to avoid the embarrassment of them not being able to get into it or, worse, out of it.

The styling of the MG Ten very cleverly camouflages the Morris Eight origins. It is rumoured that Cecil Kimber did indeed visit the Cowley drawing offices and had a hand in its flowing lines. They certainly appear to have his touch. According to other books I have read, Gerald Palmer (of the Z Magnette, Wolseley 4/44 and Riley Pathfinder) was responsible for the MG Ten body styling. He denied this in an interview with the Wolseley Register in later life. The MG's boot is bigger than the Morris 8 hp, and the MG stows the spare wheel in a compartment underneath. The bigger rear wings are fuller than the 8 hp and this means the rear doors are not interchangeable with the 8 hp due to the larger cut-out to accommodate those wings and wheel arch. This led to the rear door windows not fully winding down as their support hits that intrusion inside the door. Rear door windows on Y Types sit 1 in proud, whereas the 8-hp one drops into the door. Front doors are identical to the four-door 8 hp, as is the windscreen and sunroof. The bonnet is much longer that the 8 hp and contains a bigger Morris 10-hp engine bored out from 1,140 cc to 1,250 cc. This actually made the car a 10.9 hp, so it attracted road tax for an 11-hp car (like the later Austin Seven was 7.9 hp, so was taxed as an 8 hp). On the front was grafted the

Headlining installation on the production line at Abingdon in 1947. (BMHIT)

MG radiator grill with big, flowing wings each side in the true MG fashion. Joining the front wings to the rear wings are running boards. The 8 hp only had tumble-home sills here. So, a bit like the later MGB's modifications into the MGC, actually quite a lot of items become non-interchangeable. Photos of the MG Ten in 1938 show a mock-up of the car, and the development car was designated the EX166. MG used the 'EX' prefix on experimental models. Interestingly, it's an MG drawing office prefix and not a Morris one.

The MG Ten was fitted with a single carburettor version of the TB sports car 1,250-cc engine. This was, as mentioned, a bigger Morris Ten Series M unit. The Morris Ten four-speed gearbox was fitted with its synchromesh on the three upper gears. The Morris had its gear lever direct into the top of the gearbox, the MG Ten had it into the rear extension, and the TB used a remote selector that bolted to the MG Ten's location. If you had the right bits, you could adapt the box to fit all.

The MG Ten was a luxury car: it had leather bucket seats; a leather rear seat; Bedford cloth roof lining; carpets; it originally had the Morris Ten Bakelite instrument panel with round instruments, but later had a wooden veneer dashboard and door window surrounds; a built-in jacking 'jack-all' system; rear window blind; rear seat roof straps; rear seat centre divider; opening windscreen; electric wipers; heater and radio as extras; semaphore-trafficator indicators; reversing light; and big, chrome double-dip headlights each side of the chromium radiator grill, and a price to match it all. It was not a cheap car by any means. It was aimed at the same market as the Sunbeam Talbot Ten (a posh Hillman Minx) – the luxury end.

Production line at Abingdon in 1947. The body is being dropped onto its chassis. (BMHIT)

When the Morris Ten Series M was originally designed it had rack-and-pinion steering with parallel wishbone independent front suspension (IFS) and an anti-roll bar. The accountants were furious; this was far too expensive for a family saloon, even though the new Vauxhall Ten had independent torsion-bar front suspension. The Morris was built with the old beam-axle on leaf springs and steering box, though it did get the anti-roll bar. The TB Midget had a very similar axle, but no anti-roll bar. Before the development MG Ten EX166 was built and the chassis was modified to take this excellent IFS (designed by Alexander Issigonis along with Jack Daniels of the old MG drawing office who had been moved to Cowley) complete with the accurate rack-and-pinion steering. This system was used by MG up until 1995 when it was slightly modified. The car destined to go to that cancelled 1940 London Motor Show had this front suspension. The experimental EX166 was not actually completed until after the Second World War, its build being stopped by the hostilities.

Putting the monocoque body, which did not require a chassis, onto the strong ladder chassis led to a rather small and heavy car. While the 8-hp car had cross-bracing behind its rear seat, the MG Ten did not, perhaps to try to reduce the weight a little? With a chassis it was not required anyway. One thing that stands out immediately is the very low build of this 1930s car. This is because to keep its centre of gravity low the chassis goes underneath the rear axle, known as 'under-slung'. Even today the car's roof is often lower than the modern twenty-first-century saloons in the car park. It is 5 inches lower than the

A radiator being installed on the production line at Abingdon in 1947. (BMHIT)

Morris E and sits on an 8-ft wheelbase. The M brakes as used on the TB were fitted, which were of the single-leading-shoe type. The rear axle was that of the standard spiral-bevel Morris pattern as on the 8-hp, 10-hp and 12-hp cars. The rear axle had additional location by a Panhard rod, which stops the axle moving sideways. Front and rear suspension was fitted with the then new silent-bloc rubber bushes eliminating the old brass bearings that required greasing often. The steering column had a rubber joint fitted to help remove road vibrations from the steering wheel.

As already mentioned, the 1940 London Motor Show was cancelled. The MG Ten would have outshone the majority of Tens that still used SV engines, rod and cable brakes, beam axles and cart springs. That is, except the Vauxhall Ten. It too had an OHV engine, synchromesh gearbox and hydraulic brakes, but also a monocoque body and was available with a four-cylinder 10-hp engine or a six-cylinder 14-hp engine. The MG engine, the now famous 'XPAG', was one of the most powerful of all the 10-hp cars. In 1939, MG put the jigs and drawings into storage for a later date.

The Y Type is a design from over eighty years ago; its technology is of that era. It was a car intended for a young man driving an MG Midget sports car, who would then marry and have children but could still buy an MG that he knew well, as the Y used the same or similar components. He could service it himself, and it still had the excellent road manners of all MGs of that date. There is a poor copy of a long-lost blueprint tracing of the layout of the 'MG 10hp Series, Saloon 4 door'. Its title box tells us: 'Drawn by A.J.S.; Traced on 22.1.39; Checked by R.J. On 8.2.39.' Note the leaf-sprung axles on both ends with no shackles, but sliding boxes like the TA/TB; boot lid bottom folds into the car; the chassis front end goes over the front axle and the rear end under the rear axle.

Engine and gearbox being installed, production line at Abingdon in 1947. (BMHIT)

2

The MG Y Type, 1947–51 (YA)

The car was originally just the 'Y Type' within the company, though it kept the lengthy title of 'MG One and a Quarter Litre' on adverts in car magazines. It was 1947 before the car saw the light of day, ready for the market. It would later be called the YA once the updated YB arrived in 1951. From the start the car was dogged by its 1930s styling. By 1947 firms like Hillman, Vauxhall, Singer and others had adopted the American slab-sided look that enclosed the whole car; big flowing wings with upright radiator grills were out of fashion. Full-width styling did improve the coefficient of drag and lead to today's computer air-slippery designs. The Y's resistance to the air is high as it is a bit of a flying brick. Wind noise in the cabin is so high over 55 mph that conversation is difficult, not that many drive that fast these days with such ancient engines. Also, by the time the Y was being sold, the

The very early YA of Slater Reynolds, off-side. (Peter Veilvoye)

road tax system had become just £10 across the board and other firms were getting their 1,500-cc models ready as there was now no penalty for bigger bore engines. It eventually became the only car in its 1,200–1,300 cc old luxury 10-hp class.

March 1947 saw the first production Y Type assembled at Abingdon, then being in Berkshire. By now the government had scrapped the old horsepower tax system and introduced a blanket fee for all private cars. This meant the title of many cars using their nominated RAC horsepower was no longer relevant, so the MG Ten became the MG One and a Quarter Litre, Series Y. The first carried the chassis number Y0251 (this 251 was the phone number of the Abingdon Works). In those days all model ranges from MG began with 0251. It was up against a very good selection of the better 10-hp models, like that of Singer, Wolseley, Sunbeam-Talbot, and an 11-hp Lanchester. The Y was £280, with the cheapest (the Ford) at £195 and most expensive (the Lanchester) at £295 (all plus Purchase Tax). The chassis was built in Birmingham and transported to Abingdon by lorry. The bodies were built and painted, but not trimmed, by Nuffield Metal Products in Birmingham and again transported by lorry. All the components of the car were made by other Nuffield companies and only the trimming of the interior was done by Abingdon female employees. The Y was the first production MG to have IFS and rack-and-pinion steering, along with its strong chassis (unlike the whippy, early slim T Type Midget frames) gave the car superb handling and road manners.

As mentioned, the chassis of the Y Type was a box-section ladder type with tubular cross members. It carried all the running gear, such as the radiator-mounted right forward, with the engine behind it on rubber insulation mountings and the block being steadied by an adjustable torque rod to the offside suspension damper mounting. The gearbox was bolted directly to the crankcase at the flywheel-clutch casing (bell housing). The gearbox also sat

The very early YA of Slater Reynolds, near-side. (Peter Veilvoye)

on rubber mountings but was held down onto them by a threaded eye bolt underneath a central tube cross member. An open propeller shaft took the drive to a leaf-sprung, mounted spiral-bevel rear axle. The axle had a lever-arm damper controlling each spring. Across the car, behind the axle, was a Panhard rod. This located the axle sideways, but was only fitted to the YA and YT models (see the YA lubrication diagram, page 94). The petrol tank sat behind the rear axle, under the boot area between the chassis sides. Without a body fitted it looked odd as the rear axle appears to be on top of the chassis. This is because the chassis is 'under-slung', going under the axle to lower the car and its centre of gravity. Mounted where the driver's feet would be was the brake master cylinder, located inside a pedal box not unlike that on the Issigonis Morris Minor/1000. The foot pedals were fitted each side of the chassis section, coming up through the car's floor. The braking system was a hydraulic one, which was not common at the time but was fitted to all Nuffield cars. Bolted to the rear axle each side and just behind the front chassis IFS cross member were four jacks. The car could be jacked up using its jack-all system from a handpump under the bonnet.

The front suspension and the rack-and-pinion steering, along with the front engine mounting, were all bolted to a large steel cross member that was welded to the front of the chassis arms. The IFS had standard Morris threaded trunions on the top and bottom of the long kingpin; the lower one fixed to a triangulated spring pan and the top one to another lever-arm damper. The damper arms acted as the upper portion of the parallelogram. The steering arms ran directly from the ends of the steering rack to the steering arms bolted to

Rear view of Slater's YA.

the backs of the kingpin stub axles. The rack, acting as both steering and a track control rod, thus removed a great many joints of the worm-and-peg system of old, thence giving very little lost motion. This IFS, steering and rigid frame would give the little MG saloon excellent road manners and steering as if on rails. The Lockheed 8-inch brakes were single-leading-shoe (SLS) drum type from the Morris parts bin and identical to those on the TB-TC Midgets with a big hexagonal nut type adjusted on the back of the backplate. The handbrake was mounted between the front seats and had twin cables (again, just like the Morris Minor/1000) one to each rear drum. Adjustment of these cables was by individual locking nuts each side of the ratchet. It was not of the fly-off type fitted to the MG sports cars.

The OHV engine was the current Morris Ten series M unit modified for use in MG cars. It was bored out from the Morris's 1,140 cc to 1,250 cc. Connecting rods and crankshaft were strengthened and with bigger valves. To look at a 1,140-cc engine next to a 1,250-cc engine, they appear identical (see Chapter 5 for more detail, page 20). It is not uncommon to find a 1,140-cc engine in a Y Type or a T Type sports car as around 30,000 Morris Ten Series M were made. The XPAG in the Y only has one carburettor of the SU constant vacuum type, whereas the sports cars have twin SU carburettors. The MG saloon engine produces 46 bhp (well over its original 10-hp rating) and the T Types produce 54 bhp (brake horsepower – the engine is tested on a 'brake' to measure its power output). This little modified Morris Short Stroke Engine, as MG employees called it, was giving a very good power to capacity for its type. The engine never was a very oil-tight unit, as it was before today's neoprene sprung-lipped seals. It used some very ancient sealing systems (see Chapter 5, page 20) that is of its era.

Rear seat access to a Y – a very narrow door.

Front suicide door access to the front
bucket seats.

The gearbox is straight from the Morris M again and is used on the sports cars but with different gear lever mounting. While the internal gears are the same, that in the MG has a much longer tail shaft. There is a 7.25-in dry clutch on the flywheel and an inertia type Bendix starter motor. The car's electrics are 12 v with a Lucas dynamo and circuit breaker/voltage control box looking after the battery's charge. If you are use to modern cars with alternators, you will need to get use to a dynamo that has difficulty in maintaining a battery at nights with the lights on, windscreen wipers working and the heater motor running. (The heater was an optional extra costing £12 10s, £12.50p now.) The heater is a simple recirculatory (uses air in the car) unit and does not demist the windscreen. It can also be quite noisy.

The body of the Y Type sits on its chassis, secured by ten bolts and two tubular bracing frames at the front from the dash. The floorboards are fixed between the outer sills of the body and onto the chassis. You actually sit on the chassis on a wooden floor with the body surrounding you. There are no seat belts nor any reinforced areas to mount them. The seats are of the bucket type in the front and there is a two-seater bench seat in the rear with a central foldable armrest. The rear window has (or did have) a blind operated by the driver from a ring pull by their right ear. Above the passenger's front seat is a sunroof, which will leak onto your head if the seals are perished and the drain tubes are blocked. The windscreen opens via a central winding handle on the dash. Alas, today the correct section rubber seal for its outer edge is no longer available, so the windscreen may well leak in very heavy rain. The dash instrument board looks as if it's all wood veneer, but the wooden

Dashboard instruments are round behind an octagonal trim.

panels can be removed to reveal the steel frame underneath. The veneered panel fitted over the standard round instruments underneath has octagonal bevelled openings, making the gauges appear octagonal. The instruments are grouped around the steering column in front of the driver. Likewise, the door windows have wooden surrounds, but they screw to the steel door frames. There is a good set of instruments on view in front of the driver: oil pressure, amps, petrol contents, ignition light, speedometer, light switch, dash light switch, choke, spotlight and originally a push button starter knob that later became a pull switch. Missing is a main beam light, an engine temperature gauge and a rev counter. In 1947, there was no 'Construction and Use' regulation that insisted upon a main beam indication. When it was fitted to later cars after 1956 it was a red light, eventually becoming blue after the 1970s on all cars.

In the centre of the steering wheel, which gives a high 2.6 turns from lock to lock, is the horn push button, with a clockwork timer for the Lucas Semaphore Trafficators in each 'B' post (the centre one the door hinges are mounted on). By now many clockwork units have fallen to bits, so a Lucas indicator switch with a central red light may be screwed to the dash instead. As the steering wheel rotates there is a slip-ring arrangement under the bonnet on the column that has brass brushes inside to transfer the electrical signal to the car's wiring loom. By now the vast majority of Y Types have had flashing indicators fitted and the trafficators relegated to simple side repeaters, though not all.

The radiator is mounted in its own chromium-plated brass shell and is also braced by two rods to the body dash/firewall. This is to permit adjustment to get the bonnet's closed gaps correct. The bonnet itself is of the gull-wing type, on a central hinge and giving excellent access to all but the starter motor (this requires quite a bit of engine stripping down to get to). The cooling system is NOT pressurised; it relies on thermo-syphon (hot

Early 8-inch headlamps.

Guarantee plate on the battery box.

water rising) assisted by a centrifugal impeller water pump driven off the fan belt. Because the cooling system is not pressurised and sealed as on modern cars, the water evaporates so requires constant checking and topping up.

The headlights are mounted on a chrome tube running across between the front wings and through the radiator grill. Early cars had 8-inch units changed later to the Lucas standard 7-inch ones. They are of the modern double-dip type and today are often modified by fitting LED bulbs that use much less electrical power and so giving the battery and dynamo an easier life. Adjustment of the headlamps is by the big brass nut underneath it. Front sidelights are mounted on top of the front wings, just out of sight of the driver. Rear lights are of the 1930s 'D' type, with rear, brake and reversing bulbs. The reversing white lights only operate when the sidelights are switched on; the automatic reverse switch is on the side of the gearbox by the gear lever, under the floor. Many swap the wires to give a reversing light when the ignition is switched on. The ignition warning light is just above the steering column on the dash; it can be very dim. When new the car had a driving spotlamp fitted to the front bumper irons.

The front number plate is underneath the front bumper – ideal for hitting kerbs with and folding it back. The rear number plate is mounted on the spare wheel cover under the boot lid, with those D lamps each side giving the required white illumination at night. The carriage key to undo the locks that secure the spare wheel cover lives in a little pouch on the panel by the front passenger's feet. The starting handle, wheel brace and jacking pump handle are held in clips in the spare wheel compartment.

Car up on its jacks.

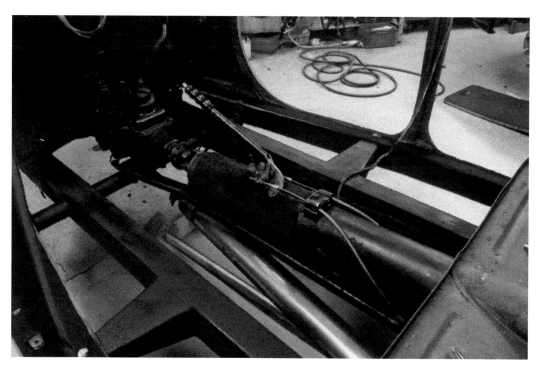

Floorboards removed to show the chassis and handbrake cables. The handbrake is very effective on a Y and can lock the rear wheels.

Spare wheel compartment, shown opened with a carriage key – note the rear reflectors.

There are hand straps above each rear seat occupant for passengers to grasp when the car is being driven in a lively manner. The rear window is quite small and has many blind spots for the rearview mirror mounted above the windscreen. The two front doors are of the suicide type, in that they are hinged at their rear edge. This requires passengers to put their bum on the seat before pulling their legs in. Rear doors are as normal, with all four doors mount on the central B post. Front seats have a limited amount of adjustment, but the steering wheel is adjustable for reach by a little thumb screw. There are ash trays each side of the windscreen and in the back of the front seats. There is no steering lock, nor servo-assisted brakes, nor power-assisted steering and a multitude of grease points that demand very regular attention.

The wheels on the YA are 16-inch with cross-ply tyres. The wheel centres are riveted to the wheel rims and not welded, so tubeless tyres cannot be fitted as the rims are not airtight. Radial ply tyres will make the steering very, very heavy and often the car will have to be moved a little to do so, such is the grip of radials. The suspension and steering are designed for 5.00 by 16-inch cross-ply tyres, but they do not give a very high mileage so many owners fit radials and suffer the arm-aching slow speed manoeuvring.

In 1948, an open-bodied version was introduced, the YT (for Tourer), and this car was intended for export only. It was designed with the ability to be left-hand drive (LHD). This meant the battery box under the bonnet on top of the dash/firewall had to be moved from the nearside to a central position. As the YT uses the front body panels of the YA, the YA had the central battery as well. This unfortunately put the battery under the bonnet's central hinge, requiring the bonnet to be removed to fit a new battery.

Steering wheel adjustment.

UK specification air silencer.

Export specification oil bath air cleaner.

The YA and YT use the majority of their mechanical components from the MG TC and as there is a thriving club scene for MG Midgets, such spares are easy to find. However, body parts for all Y Types are very scarce and sometimes unavailable. The body, chassis and batch numbers are under the bonnet. On the near side of the battery box is a brass guarantee plate with the original engine number and the chassis number. Very near this plate, but on the dash, is the body batch number. This is not the chassis number, but unfortunately it has been used on some logs books when local councils did car registration. The chassis number is repeated and stamped into the front near side chassis panel where the steering rack goes through it. This can be hard to read. The engine number is stamped on a plate either on the bell housing or on the offside under the exhaust manifold. Engine and chassis numbers are unique to the car, though many cars will have had numerous engines fitted over the years so that on the brass plate may not be the one now fitted (see Chapter 5 for more). A total of 6,158 YAs were made; 326 were LHD. This does not include the YT numbers, even though the chassis numbering was continuous through both models so its hard to identify a YT from a chassis number alone.

There is a headlamp dip switch fitted on the floor for the driver's left foot and the instrument board was not very ergo dynamic, as all the switches looked the same.

The YA of 1947 was quite a good performer, getting from a standing start to 50 mph in just 16.5 seconds, whereas the majority of 10-hp cars of that date took an average of 22 seconds. The car's maximum speed was clocked at 69 mph taken over two opposite runs by *The Motor* magazine, and it managed an average miles per gallon of 27. The YA

YB lower wishbone with anti-roll bar and lowered inner mounting and the car sits lower.

was normally available in a two-tone colour scheme, which was easily done as it was the bolted-on panels that were the other colour, i.e. the front and rear wings and running boards. The wheels were originally the two colours as well. The YA was priced at £525 and with Purchase Tax it sold for £672 – twice that of a 10-hp Ford Popular. In the first few years of the YA most went for export, with many going to Australia.

Nothing on the car is computerised; everything is either mechanical or electro-mechanical. You, the driver, are the management systems; you operate the choke, not an engine-sensing device. You are the power steering and the brake servo. This means that if the car falters on the road, providing you have a bit of knowledge, most minor faults can be fixed in a lay-by – no need to call out a recovery lorry. You will quickly know what tool kit and spares to carry.

YA lower wishbone with no anti-roll bar or lowered inner mounting and the car sits higher.

3

MG YT Tourer, 1948–50

Between the two world wars there had been a rise in the popularity of open-topped touring cars in Britain. Even though this country had such inclement weather, nearly all the car makers had rag-top models alongside the standard ones. MG was no exception as its sports cars were all open-topped anyway. It was the very, very few closed models that were the rarity, which were usually built by specialist coach makers for customers. The two big family sporting saloons, the VA and SA/WA (the WA followed the SA after that car had had so many modifications), were sent to Salmons & Sons of Newport Pagnell to have that company's 'Sunshine Roof' fitted. This was a very clever hood that was folded down or erected via a big hand-worked handle on the nearside of the boot lid.

Peter's YT off-side. (Peter Veilvoye)

The MG Y Type's open-topped model was assembled at Abingdon alongside the YA. Oddly, the YT's body was built by Morris Bodies Branch and not Nuffield Metal Products, though they did supply some pressings.

As already mentioned, the YT was built from 1948 using the YA as its basis. Around 877 were made, ceasing in 1950 as the car was not proving popular. It was originally meant for export only, but quite a few were sold in the UK and today many are reimported from the USA. The main difference from the four door, six-light YA saloon was the lack of a roof, with it only having two doors with big elbow cut-outs and being fitted with the more powerful twin-carburettor engine of the MG TC Midget. Instead of having 46 bhp to power it along, it had 54 bhp. It was not much faster though, as with the hood down its coefficient of drag was higher than the saloon. The idea hankered after the pre-war open-topped cars. Hillman did the same, as did Rover and Vauxhall (though to cut off the roof they both used Tickfords of Newport Pagnell, as Salmons became after the war).

The bonnet, radiator grill, front wings, rear wings, engine firewall, rear panels and boot lid were the same as the YA, as was all the running gear and chassis. But it was a two-door car and they were built up on an ash frame with steel panels pinned on. The two wide doors hinged at their rear edge so were termed 'suicide doors'. Access to a narrower rear seat was by the front seats tipping forward. The hood and its framing folded down around the rear seat and the side panels were stored behind the seat squab. The top of the dash

Jerry Birkbeck's YT in use.

behind the windscreen had two humps, like the TC sports car. The car was not renowned for its watertightness. The YT had a very similar instrument panel to the TC sports cars, and its windscreen could also fold flat. The windscreen wipers of the YT were mounted atop the windscreen, whereas the saloons YA and YB had their motor under the bonnet and the wipers in the top of the dash. The YT looks like a big four-seater TD Midget.

The instrument information on the dash was the same as the TC – again with no engine temperature gauge. The speedometer was set in front of the passenger with the tachometer (rpm gauge) in front of the driver. Three small instruments between the two bigger ones gave fuel contents, ammeter and oil pressure. There was no clockwork indicator selector switch in the steering wheel boss as on the YA, but those for the USA had the interrupter-type flashing indicators that used the front side lights and the rear brake lights, being white at the front and red at the rear. This was quite legal in the UK well up until about 1956 when the Construction and Use regulations caught up with 'flashers' and insisted they be amber and put a flashing speed of between 60 and 120 per minute. MGAs had the interrupter-type flashers for the USA market as well.

Today, due to their rareness, the YT model fetches very high prices, being one of the scarce models of the MG factory. Having one restored is also very expensive due to the

Jerry's YT dashboard. Note the speedometer in in front of the passenger.

type of construction of the body. Oddly, only 251 were LHD. It was the fact that the YT was made to be LHD or RHD with little effort that the TD Midget, which followed it some months later, could be sold in the USA as a LHD car. Not only was the Y Type the first production MG with independent front suspension, it was also the first one available as left-hand drive.

The much later craze of fitting the MGB engine to the Y Type is difficult. As the MGB uses what is essentially the Y's suspension and steering, it should be an easy job; however, it isn't as the steering column of the Y ends up going 'through' the BMC 'B' series distributor.

A total of 325 YTs went to Australia, it being the best export market for the car. On Australian roads the Luvax-Girling lever-arm dampers were to prove very short-lived. Many were modified to take telescopic dampers instead with the control valve removed from the lever arm units, converting them to just upper suspension wish bones.

Jerry's YT with the hood up.

4

The MG YB, 1951–53

In 1951, the YA was updated. In 1948, a TC body tub was put loosely onto a YA chassis at Abingdon, just to see how it looked. The Y chassis was shortened by 5 inches for this exercise. As the YA's chassis was a far better one than that of the current TC Midget, it was to be modified to suit the sports cars and also standardise more components, thus reducing costs. At the same time the opportunity was taken to update the sports cars with twin-leading-shoe (TLS) brakes from Lockheed, a bigger clutch and improved flywheel and starter motor. The wheels were to be cheaper and smaller pressed steel ones of 15-inch dia, with spoked wheels as an extra. The 'TD' chassis was to have its rear end made 'over-slung' and shortened by 5 inches as it was only a two seater. The pedal box was moved a little rearwards as the driver would be further back.

Rear view of my YB.

Off-side front view of my YB.

Leather front bucket seats.

The original TD Midget was then assembled at Abingdon with no initial design work or drawings and then going into production in August 1949. The ancient Morris spiral-bevel rear axle was replaced with the new stronger Nuffield hypoid gear axle and the Girling removable brake drums with a cast one-piece hub and drum brake.

It was then obvious to update the YA using the better TLS brakes of the TD along with all the other modifications, and in 1951 the YB was born. To the untrained eye the YB looks identical to the YA, until you know where to look. To cope with the smaller 15-inch wheels the rear wings of the YB have a deeper section, and this is by far the easiest way of identifying a YA from a YB. The rear Panhard rod was deleted and an anti-roll bar fitted to the front suspension to cure a rather tail-happy car that over-steered if driven hard. The front suspension geometry was also altered by dropping the lower inner-spring-pan's mountings by 2 inches. This beam can be seen welded to the cross member and does not appear on any other model using this system. The YA, YB, YT, TD, TF, MGA and MGB all used variations of this 1939 Issigonis IFS, right up to the ventilated, power-assisted disc-braked 1991 MG RV8.

The YB now had Girling TLS drum brakes. With the smaller 15-inch wheels went a combined drum and wheel hub, which had different wheel nut spacings, making wheels between YA/YT no longer interchangeable with the YB. Wheels now also needed to be

Rear seat with central arm rest.

XPAG engine with dynamo, showing the jackall pump on the firewall with its reservoir on the battery box, confusing MOT examiners who think it is a brake fluid reservoir.

fitted, with the hole cut in the centre that lined up with the hole in the brake drum, as this car has snail cone shoe adjusters inside the drum. The different rear axle differential unit had a longer nose, so the prop-shaft of a YB is shorter. The electrical system had a different Lucas control/cut-out unit, now with a separate fuse box. There were fewer grease nipples to attend to as the YB's wheel bearings were not fitted with them, the front ones being packed with grease in a small hub cap and the rear ones being lubricated by the differential hypoid gear oil. So, the update of the YA to the YB was mostly hidden mechanical items and, as mentioned, they both look almost identical. The TLS brakes did improve the car's stopping ability over the rather wooden action of the older SLS ones. The car went round corners even better now the suspension geometry had been modified and it was a little faster – by 2 mph. The YB's smaller wheels bought the car into line with the majority of other 1,200–1,500-cc saloons on the UK market, who nearly all used 5.2-inch by 15-inch cross-ply tyres. Fitting modern radials, as on the YA/YT, require inner tubes as the wheel centres are riveted to the rims, not welded. The YB's wheels have a much bigger wheel nut spacing, so they cannot be used on the earlier cars. When the original MG TD Midget had steel wheels there was an outcry by the enthusiasts, so spoked wheels were made available. With the correct splined hubs, these can be fitted to the YB as well.

Single carburettor with later heatshield and rerouted petrol pipe to avoid the hot exhaust manifold. Hot weather causes airlocks in the fuel pipes with modern petrol.

YB wings removed showing the independent front suspension.

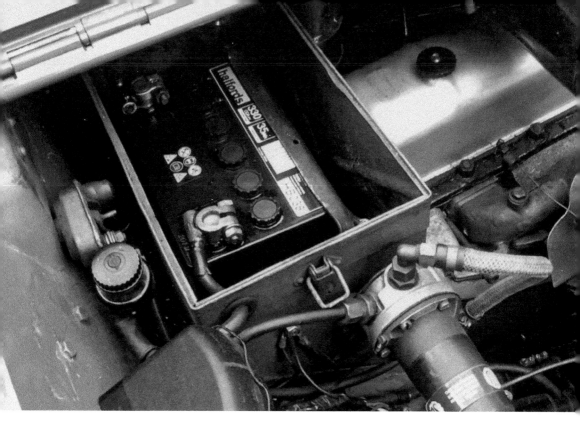

Later central battery box that requires the bonnet removing to change it. Note the battery isolation switch on the starter motor solenoid.

The YB sits a little lower at the front end compared to a YA and its slightly different rear axle ratio (5.143 YA to 5,125 of the YB) with the smaller wheels gave slightly better acceleration, though top speeds were almost identical. The spare wheel cover was slightly deeper on the YB as its tyres were of a bigger section.

By 1953 when the last YB was built, production was at a trickle. No one wanted what was a 1930s-styled car when the American full-width look was all the rage. Only 1,301 were made. Few were exported and only one was LHD. The majority were also only one colour; few were two-tone. The YB was priced at £989 with purchase tax and this put it almost as expensive as some 14-hp models. Dick Jacobs ran a YB in races and had some success; the car still exists.

Above and below: Deep YB rear wing compared to the much shallower right wing. Easiest way to determine which model you are looking at.

The much wider-spaced five-stud 15-in YB wheel.

16-in YA/YT wheels studs are much closer together. (Peter Veilvoye)

5

The XPAG Engine, 1939–56

The 'Morris Ten Short-Stroke Engine', as Abingdon called the 1,250-cc OHV unit fitted to the 1939 MG TB, has its own story. The Y Type uses this famous engine, and a good dollop of information will prove useful to any Y owner.

In the UK there are many modern car owners who would be amazed to realise their all-aluminium alloy V8 engine fitted to their Rover dates back to the USA and was designed in the 1950s. I refer to the General Motors 215-cu-in engine as fitted to the Buick Skylark, Special, Pontiac Tempest and Oldsmobile F85 Cutlass. The rights to remanufacture this family sedan engine by Rover dates back to 1965. It was seen later in the MGB GT V8. Similarly, there are lots of overseas owners of MGs who would be amazed to realise that the engine they thought was exclusively an MG product was in fact borrowed from a staid, mass-produced Morris saloon car.

Single-carburettor engine of the YA and YB.

Twin-carburettor engine of the YT.

In 1935, the small MG factory in Abingdon, Berkshire (now Oxfordshire), England, had a bit of a shock. While the company had been doing well on the British racing circuits with their fast Little British Cars, production had become a rather ragged discipline. The company had been subjected to an internal reorganisation and had been sold to the Nuffield Group. MG had been the personal property of William Morris, but his vast emporium had now got him into trouble with the UK income tax department, hence the new arrangements. This meant that now MG came under the management of the Nuffield directors. The senior manager who was now in control of MG was one Leonard Lord, who did not agree with 'wasting time and money on racing cars'. Companies exist to make profits for their shareholders, not to squander it on playing games, was the view of the new management.

Along with MG now having to drop many of their less-profitable lines from the numerous models and variations they listed, was a decree that all MGs must now use in-house corporate components. This resulted in the tiny OHC MG Midgets and various four- and six-cylinder specials stopping production. Kimber was not too worried as he had long sought to get MG upmarket with big, fast, well-appointed saloon cars and the results of this aim were the very elegant six-cylinder SA and later the WA. The VA, with its four-cylinder engine was a bit dumpy, but affordable. Under the skins of these cars were components straight from the Nuffield production lines of the Morris and Wolseley saloons. Morris were nearly always side-valve (SV) driven, with Wolseley using overhead-valve (OHV) conversions of the same engines. The family of engines from the

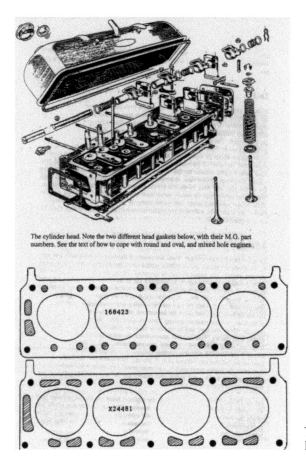

The cylinder head. Note the two different head gaskets below, with their M.G. part numbers. See the text of how to cope with round and oval, and mixed hole engines.

The two different cylinder head gaskets.

Morris Engine Branch were all inter-related. Many parts were common to them all, such as the tappet blocks with four cam followers in, two sets to a four cylinder, three to a six. Connecting rods, cam profiles, valves, guides and pistons were all common. Even the stroke of many Nuffield/Morris engines dated back to that historic British car of 102 mm, the Morris Bull Nose Oxford and Cowley saloon. The basic engines in the SA and WA were straight from the Wolseley 18/80 range, and that for the VA was from the Wolseley 12/48. That of the Wolseley 12/48 refers to 12-hp range with 48 bhp. The 12 hp refers to the road taxation group for the Exchequer, not the actual engine power. Common sizes in the 1930s for UK cars were 7 hp, 8 hp, 10 hp, 12 hp, 14 hp and 18 hp, and road tax was charged based on this. The horsepower tax was ancient, devised by the Royal Automobile Association, or RAC, earlier in the century when engines were feeble and it used the bore but ignored the stroke – hence the number of small-bore UK engines. Unusually for Morris, the equivalent to the Wolseley 12/48 also had an OHV engine. This Morris was called a 12/4, meaning 12 hp and four cylinder just to be awkward. Next down the range of the Nuffield line-up was the Morris 10/4, a 10-hp car with four cylinders. The Wolseley equivalent was the 12/40, 12 hp with 40 bhp. For the uninitiated, Wolseleys were always the better equipped version of the more mundane cooking Morris. The Morris 10/4 was about to become part of the MG empire in a similar manner to that of the first MG. I doubt if any Morris or Wolseley

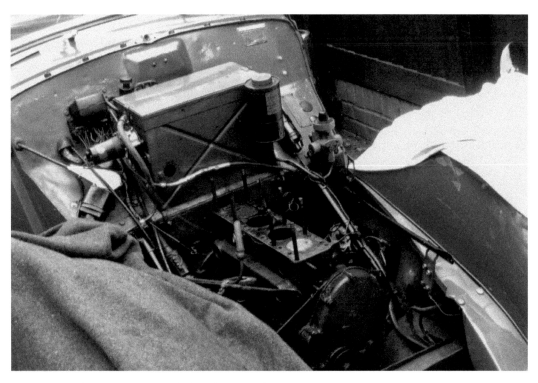

Engine being prepared to be lifted out. Radiator removed.

New 0.060-inch oversize pistons used in my YB engine.

then was ever exported to the USA, as they were far too British. These two makes will not be familiar to Americans, but MG relied heavily on their components. Morris, Wolseley, MG and Riley made up the Nuffield Group. MG and Riley were two very small parts; Morris, however, was massive. Along with Austin, they were then the two biggest UK car manufacturers.

Due to the decree of Leonard Lord banning small-scale specialist component runs, from 1935 MG were forced to use the running gear of the Morris 10/4 in their new sports car. Brakes, steering, instruments, engine, gearbox, axles, etc., were all Morris 10/4 Series 3 components. The engine was of a very long 102-mm stroke, dating back to veteran Morris days with a 63.5-mm bore with a cork clutch running in oil. Not a good recipe for a sports car engine. The five-port cylinder head was a casting adapted to what had originally been a side-valve unit. The engine was slow to accelerate, with poor breathing, and had poor top end performance. It was never intended to be a sports car unit and only fate had put it into the 1936 MG TA Midget. It was reliable enough, however, and a good saloon car engine for a workhorse, but it was too heavily built for a 1935 new MG model. Its ancestry dated back to 1923, and even further to the Hoshkiss-built Morris engine of the Bull Nose.

While MG were busy getting the TA into production and pleased the engine was of 1292 cc (bigger than the tiny overhead camshaft 847-cc engines), Morris Engines were about to announce a better unit. The extra capacity made up for the poorer bhp per litre. For some time Morris had been looking at their engine range. It needed a full redesign. All of the range were developments of much older units and it was time to invest in bettering them. The first group of cars to get an improved engine was the 10 and 12 horsepower range. These were the most common size of car sold in the UK. Like any large company, no single person designed anything from scratch, as that was far too expensive to put into production. Items had to be carried over as and when suitable. In the Morris Engines design office was a young man who had come from the Anzani Engine Factory and built aircraft engines. He was obviously talented so was given the task of improving the M series of engines. This M series was the MPJM in the Morris 10/4, the MPJW in the Wolseley 10/40 Series 2, and the MPJG in the MG TA; in fact, all the 10-hp series. He was Claud Bailey, and his updated and improved engine was to be fitted into the then new chassisless Morris Ten Series M saloon (sedan). (Do not muddle up the chassis designation M with the earlier engine series M.) The new engine was designated the Morris X series of engines and they were of 90-mm stroke with a 63.5-mm bore. Note the bore: it meant the same pistons could be used again and the machinery for boring the cylinders, as in the TA engine. The X series was not a new engine, but an improved one. It was of 1,140 cc with a modern dry clutch.

As the XPJM in the new Morris Ten series M and the XPJW in the Wolseley 10/40 Series 3 the engine took to the roads in 1938. By 1947 over 80,000 Morris Ten series M had been produced, along with 12,000 Wolseley 10/40s. During the Second World War the engine was built and fitted to tens of thousands of utility units as petrol/electric sets, water pumps, etc., for use by the armed forces. These can be identified by their prefix of XPJM/U. All these engines will also fit into the MG models that used the X series. By 1939 the engine had been developed into a 10.9-hp unit. It emerged with 1,250 cc with a 90-mm stroke and a 66.5-mm bore. This was a bored out 1,140-cc XPJM unit, but not quite. It had a stronger crankshaft, connecting rods and pistons. The head had larger valves and it was a real sweet running, easily revved unit. It went into the MG TB along with the improved Morris Series

46

Rocker shaft fitted. Note the deflector over I and 2 rockers, which stops the oil leak from the filler cap.

Cylinder block being bored. (Headline Engineering, Wavendon)

M improved gearbox with remote control. It was not used in a Morris 12-hp model, as that range was dropped as the Series M Ten was very popular and selling well.

Claud Bailey had done a good job. His improved X series of engines stopped being used by Morris and Wolseley in 1948. Morris went back to SV units and many Wolseleys got large OHC units. But MG continued using the engine and improving it until 1955. One Wolseley used it from 1952 until 1956 as the XPAW. After the Second World War, in 1945, the XPAG 1,250-cc engine was put into the TC Midget, then in 1947 into the new Y and YT sports saloons. In 1949, It was seen in the new TD Midget and by 1952 in the improved YB saloon. By 1953 it had been bored out to 1,466 cc in the TF Midget. In 1952, Wolseley had used the engine in their 4/44 (four cylinder, 44 bhp). This car looks just like a taller version of the 1953 MG ZA saloon – both are closely related. However, the Z series saloons used an Austin engine of the BMC 'B' series.

As well as those X series used in Morris and Wolseley cars and all those utility engines, MG used quite a number. There were 379 in the TB, 10,000 in the TC, 28,643 in the TD, 1,022 in the TD Mk 2, 6,200 in the TF, 6,158 in the YA; 1,301 in the YB, 877 in the YT, and 34,000 in the Wolseley 4/44. That in the 4/44 being a car not exported to the USA used the basic SC2 engine of the YB (SC meaning single carburettor). The grand total of the engine's

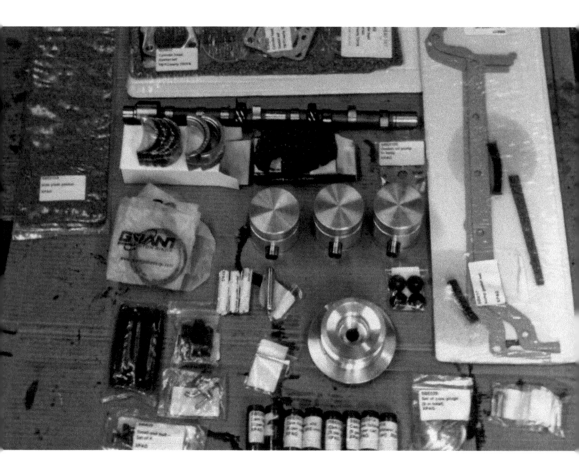

Bits required for an XPAG rebuild, note one piston is at the machine shop for checking the bores.

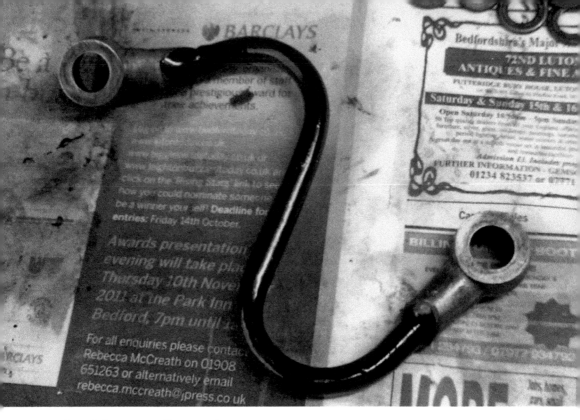

One of the copper oil pump pipes

production is in the region of 186,600, not including those made as spares or for the war utility kits. The 1,140-cc engine can easily be bored out to 1,250 cc, but not 1,466 cc, which had required a re-core to move the cylinder centres.

Claud Bailey had lowered the reciprocating mass, improved the breathing, fitted larger valves with better porting, counter-balanced everything, fitted full-flow oil filtration, shortened the stroke and designed in very modern cooling with water flow only through the head with the cylinder block using thermo-syphon. In the 1,250 cc he strengthened it all and produced a real winner. There was a smaller version of 918 cc that was used in the Wolseley Eight, 918 cc being the older Morris 8-hp engine standard size, but few were ever made. Claud went on to join the design team of another very famous X series of engines in the late 1940s when he moved to Jaguar. That was the Jaguar six-cylinder, twin OHC XK series used in the E types and sports saloons.

XPAG Technical Data, Modifications List and Casting Numbers

The TC was the first with a timing chain tensioner. The earlier engines had a 7 ¼-in clutch. The Wolseley 4/44 (change of system now, four cylinder with 44 bhp,) engine is really an SC/2 with a different sump casting.

49

Engine Codes
1936 to 1956
(Consists of four letters, followed by the engine's number)

(1) Model	(2) Valves	(3) Bore and hp	(4) Make
U Morris 8	S Sidevalve	H 57 mm, 8 hp	M Morris
M Morris 10/4	P OHV	J 63.5 mm, 10hp	G MG
X late Morris 10/4	C OHC	A 66.5 mm, 11 hp	W Wolseley
T Morris 12/4		B 69.5 mm, 12 hp	C Commercial
Q 2 ltr, 6 cyl		E 72 mm, 13 hp	U Utility
O 3.5 ltr, 6cyl		D 75 mm, 14 hp	
		D 61.5 mm, 6 cyl	
		H 69 mm, 6cyl	

Examples				
Model	Bore/Stroke	Type	cc	Made
Morris 10/4 s 'M'	63.5 by 90 OHV	XPJM	1,140	1938–48
Morris 10/4 Ultiity		XPJM/U	1,140	1939–45
Wolseley Ten s3		XPJW	1,140	1939–48
MG TC Midget	66.5 by 90 OHV	XPAG	1,250	1939
MG TC Midget		XPAG		1945–49
MG TC Midget		XPAG/TD		1949–52
MG TD Mk 2		XPAG/TDC		1949–52
MG TD 8-in clutch		XPAG/TD2		1952–53
MG YA		XPAG/SC		1947–52
MG YA 8-in clutch		XPAG/SC2		1951
MG YB		XPAG/SC2		1952–53
MG YT LHD		XPAG/TL		1948–50
MG YT RHD		XPAG/TR		1948–50
MG TF Midget		XPAG/TF		1953–55
Wolseley 4/44		XPAW		1953–56
MG TF 1500	72 by 90	XPEG	1,466	1953–55

Casting Numbers

These can be found on the cylinder block behind the dynamo or on top of the head. Because of the huge numbers of these X Series engines used in the late 1940s and 1950s, many items will have been swapped about, especially when in the 1960s and 1970s owners were looking for bits in scrap yards. There are a few Y Types about fitted with Morris Ten Series M 1,140-cc engines, sometimes unknown to the car's present owner. Casting numbers stand proud of the casting's surface and are not stamped into the metal. If the number is stamped in it is probably a serial number.

Model/Item	Casting No.
Early Morris/Wolseley Ten 1140cc 'X' cylinder block, oval	22500
Later post-war 1,140-cc cylinder block, oval water holes	24144
Early MG 1,250-cc 'X' block, octagon cast in, oval water holes	24146
Later post-war 1,250-cc MG block, octagon cast in, oval holes	24445
4/44, later TD and TF block, no octagon, round water holes	168421
Early 1,140-cc cylinder-head, no centre oil drain, oval water holes	22812
Early pre-war 1,140-cc head, with round holes	22952
Later post-war 1,140-cc head, same as early 'T' type, oval holes	22952
Later TD, Y oval-hole cylinder head, short-reach plug	22952
4/44, TD and TF head, round water holes, long-reach plugs	168422
Late 4/44 head, round water holes	168425

Note: With the 22952 head's use MG one had bigger valves.

The core plug hidden at the rear of the cylinder block.

Casting numbers are often quite rough: with the pattern getting knocked about with use and age, numbers can be difficult to read. On the cylinder block it is under the tappet cover, behind the dynamo, above the octagon if the block has one. On the head it is easy to see on the top, though often not fully clear, casting 'flash' obscuring it. 'Round' and 'oval' refer to the coolant holes in the head/block face.

There is a full modification list by engine numbers on the MGCC Y Register website under MG Engine History, XPAG section – details in Chapter 9.

XPAG in Use

This 1930s Morris engine is well known for being oily. This is because it is a 1930s design and uses ancient methods of sealing. There is a mountain of information on this engine on the websites (see page 95) under 'MG Engines 1938–1991' written by me, but here are a few pointers towards its use today.

The engine has core plugs dotted over the block and head. They are used in the casting process to support the core of the engine's cooling voids (water jacket), the place the water flows through to cool the engine. Once the new casting is to be machined, there will be holes into the coolant areas where the core supports were. These are machined out with a tidy edge and steel discs called core plugs that are convexed are fitted. Most are easy to get to in situ, except for one. This one is at the rear of the cylinder block and on the Y hard up against the bulkhead under the battery box. Murphy's Law says that it will always be this one that will leak. The steel core plugs corrode with age, mild steel being a quite unstable metal in this respect if an anti-corrosion additive is not used. If you do not know the age of your core plugs, change this one if you get the opportunity.

On the early engines the oil pipes feed from the pump to the filter, then from the filter to the block. Late engines have no pipes as they have drillings inside the casting. The two pipes are made of copper; however, copper age hardens, and the older it is the more brittle it becomes. Engineers who own XPAG-powered cars will remove those pipes and anneal them at regular intervals. Now that the XPAGs are an ancient bit of engineering it is well worth removing those pipes and fitting a flexible pipe conversion made of stainless-steel hoses. The copper pipes can split at any time and if you miss the sudden drop in oil pressure on the gauge, the engine will seize up solid in a few yards.

The valve gear on the XPAG is very noisy. Depending upon the camshaft fitted the tappet gaps can be either 0.019 in or 0.012 in (19 thou or 12 thou). Do not believe the little brass plaque on the rocker cover if it says 19 thou, as by now your engine will have gone through 2 or 3 cams (they are infamous for wearing out on the lobes). In the book on the website mentioned above is a method of checking which cam you have. Be warned that if you run an XPAG with the rocker cover off, you will be soaked in oil as the oil jets from the rockers face up onto the cover then it deflects down onto the valves to lubricate and cool them.

The big round air filter that sits across the engine is no such thing on the European market cars; it is just an air silencer. Only export cars have proper oil bath air filters. These are a big saucepan shaped thing fitted by the side of the carburettor and require regular cleaning and oil changes.

Early water pump with a grease nipple – current ones made in India do not have one.

The head casting number on the manifold side, an accurate way to check which you have.

There are three different lengths of fan belt. The belt is a very thick one used on pre-Second World War cars, unlike the slim one used on post-1953 MGs with BMC engines.

The rear crankshaft oil sealing on the XPAG, like many others of its day, is a mechanical one. You cannot actually fit a new seal. It is a version of the way water was lifted out of the River Nile in Egypt in 100 BC – an Archimedes' screw. It's a scroll cut into the crankshaft running in a close tolerance hole with just 0.003-in clearance. As the crank rotates it literally screws the oil back in. Alas, as the engine wears the oil flow increases until eventually the scroll cannot cope and you get the famous drip from the hole at the bottom of the clutch bell housing. Most owners fit a drip tin that they empty from time to time. It saves annoying friends by dropping oil on their clean driveways. The front seal is crushed asbestos string, but this leaks eventually as well.

The book to get if you wish to tune your XPAG is *Tuning and Maintenance of MGs* by Phillip Smith, printed by Foulis.

The most dangerous thing you can do with an XPAG is to use the starting handle incorrectly. Put all your fingers and thumbs on the same side as you grip it, otherwise a kickback may break a thumb. Turn the engine over slowly until you are past compression, then swing the handle hard round.

6

The Gearbox, Suspension and Rear Axle

The running gear of the TB, TC, TD, TF, YA, YB, YT and Wolseley 4/44 is all based on that humble saloon car, the 1939 Morris Ten. That includes the gearbox, but there are a few differences between the model's gearboxes that makes them all easily identifiable from the others. The actual gearbox and the bell housings are all almost identical (though ratios do differ on the 'intermediate' gears – first, second and third). It is the bolt-on bits that tell you from which car the gearbox came. The Morris Ten Series M gearbox looks just like any MG version, but the gear lever comes directly out of the top cover of the gearbox. The

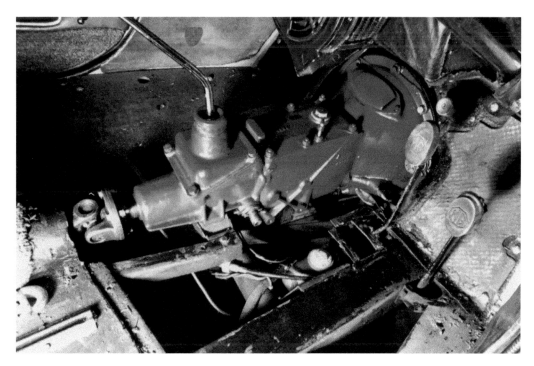

The removed the gearbox requires the front seats being taken out and the wooden floor lifting.

The gearbox is held down by an eye bolt. The cast-iron lug is often broken.

rear casing is also very short, so if you tried to fit it to your Y Type, the prop-shaft would be about a foot too short. That fitted to the 'T' series is again almost identical to the Morris version, but instead of the gear lever coming out of the top of the gearbox, a rear-extension gear change linkage is fitted to the top of the gearbox. This puts the gear lever much further back than in a Y Type, so again there would be problems trying to fit it. The Y Type version is like the Morris one, but with a plain cover on the top of the gearbox. In the Y Type the gear-selector rods are longer and extend out of the rear of the gearbox casing into a much longer rear extension. The gear change lever fits into this rear extension, so it is not like either the T Series or the Morris gearbox, though the T Series does have a very similar rear-extension casting.

That in the Wolseley 4/44 would give you a major headache as it looks exactly like the Y type, but there is nowhere to fit the gear lever. There are rods sticking out of the offside for a steering column-change linkage and the internals are on their side. However, most of the bearings, gears, etc., are interchangeable between all boxes in sets.

The weaknesses of this gearbox is its synchromesh and that the first and reverse gears are direct gear selection (first and reverse use the same gears). The synchromesh wears so one has to learn to double-de-clutch to get smooth downwards changes. Whatever you do never try to engage first or reverse with the car moving; do it stationary. This is because the gear selectors are not trying to engage lugs on the sides of the constant mesh second, third and fourth, assisted by the synchronising of the two gear's speeds with the synchromesh cones. Instead, you are moving the actual gear itself into engagement with another – one stationary and the other spinning

A broken lug. A repair is on the MGCC Y Register website.

The most common cause of poor gear change and jumping out of gear is loose locking bolts on the selectors. Tighten up and lock with steel wire. (Ted Gardener)

round if the car is moving. It is much safer to have these two gears not moving, otherwise it's very possible to break a tooth off the first gear on the layshaft. Currently, no one is making new layshafts. Also, if the gearbox jumps out of gear on lifting the accelerator or is very difficult to select a gear, suspect the locking bolts on the gear selector rods. These are wire-locked with copper wire. Copper age hardens, so it eventually crumbles and the bolts loosen off. It's not difficult to fix as just by removing the top cover on the gearbox you can see them, tighten them up and re-wire-lock with steel wire. The original oil seals at each end of the gearbox were initially leather; by now they will be rock hard and leak unless later neoprene ones from Moss have been fitted. The spring under the gear lever often breaks with old age, but new ones are cheap and easy to fit. If your gear lever is really sloppy, it is a broken spring.

Rear axles on the YA/YT are the old 1930s Morris spiral-bevel banjo type (as its casing looks like a banjo) and they do suffer from weak half-shafts. The 1950s Nuffield hypoid-bevel axle on the YB is much stronger. Both suffer from oil leaking onto the brake linings if the seals are worn. Parking on a sideways slope can cause this. Loose 'U' bolts holding the axle to the leaf springs can chatter and wear into the axle tubes. Bolted to the axle are the two rear jacks of the built-in jack-all system. In old age these can get very rusty and fail to retract, requiring assistance from a bit of wood. New seals are available from the MGOctCC and the MGCC Y Register website has articles in this. The jack-all handpump is under the bonnet on the nearside with its reservoir bolted to the battery box. MOT testers

Trying to engage first or reverse with the car moving can snap off a tooth from the layshaft. This shows a failed attempt to weld it back on.

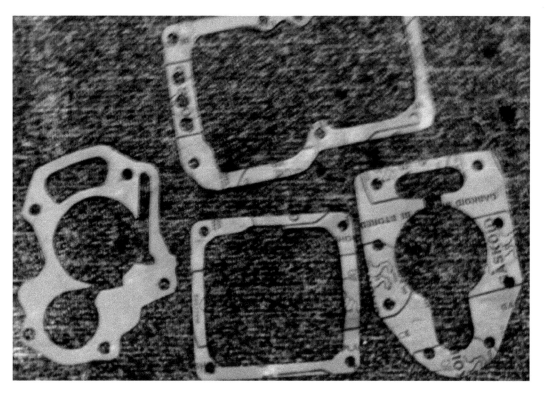

You will have to make your own gaskets for the gearbox.

often confuse this as the brake master cylinder reservoir, which is actually under the driver's floor under a little removable panel, like the Morris 1000.

The gearbox is held down onto its rear rubber mounts by an eye bolt as mentioned. The lug cast into the gearbox sometimes breaks away, leaving the box free to move about. The first sign is the gear lever wobbling a lot and hitting your knee as you go over bumps, potholes and sleeping policemen. It is repairable, though – see details on page 56.

There are two sizes of clutch fitted to the Y: originally the YA/YT had a 7.25-in one and the YB an 8-in one. But by now, with engines and gearboxes having been swapped about, you would need to remove it to see what size your car has. Then there is the catch 22 problem: what if someone has fitted the YB's gearbox to a YA, or vice versa? The first motion shaft (the one the clutch plate sits on) is ¾-in diameter on the YA's gearbox and 7/8-in diameter on the YB's gearbox. But the flywheel on the engine will be drilled for the original size clutch. It is lucky that that from the 1950s Hillman Minx has the ¾-in centre on a 7.25-in diameter clutch plate. Ensure you fit a new clutch plate with the 'Engine Side' stamping facing the flywheel.

The top leaf of the rear springs can, in old age, be worn by the clips that keep the leaves together. This put a groove in a highly stressed item, and from the groove a crack can grow until the leaf breaks. The front suspension's top trunion on the kingpin, the one that the lever arm Luvax-Girling damper is on, requires very frequent greasing. The lower

Jackall pump with its removable handle. Behind the handle is the body number plate. The chassis and engine numbers are on the plate on the battery box.

Front jacks are bolted to the chassis; the rear to the back axle.

one also needs greasing, but it's the top one that can seize up and shear the big bolt that passes through it joining it to the damper arms. The first sign is a high-pitched squeak as you bounce the car. It also shows up as rusty dust around the bolt's head and nut; this is the bolt wearing away as it is being twisted in its housing. Should it break, it could be disastrous. The whole front suspension and steering require greasing every 500 miles anyway, but today owners fail to read the servicing book, assuming the Y is like their modern car and sealed for life. It is not.

The Nuffield axle and the YB half-shaft – very different to the YA.

7

YA or YB? That is the Question

It is not hard to pick up a copy of a motoring article on the New MG One and a Quarter Litre Saloon. The press have always printed full road tests and technically detailed articles on new models. So if you want to find out about your YA today you can buy booklets from Brooklands Books entitled *MG 'Y' Types & Magnette ZA/ZB* (ISBN 1-85520-347-2). YAs, YTs and ZAs abound in its ninety-two pages of old article reprints, but there is very little on the YB or even ZB. By the time MG came to update these cars, the news was not so important, especially if very little external differences could be seen on the updated or face-lifted model. For we enthusiasts, this leads to many people not even knowing there was an updated Y series – the YB. There are even fewer who know how to tell them apart from the YA. Worse is the fact that MG themselves did not add the relevant updated bits until quite a few YBs had been built. The press would rather show a face-lift as news; hidden, updated items are not as interesting or newsworthy.

As strange as it may seem, the YA carried over some rather ancient engineering from pre-war Morris models. Though the YA (I call it the YA, though it was simply the Y until the inception of the YB) had rack-and-pinion steering with independent front suspension (IFS) it still had single-leading-shoe (SLS) front brakes. The IFS and steering put the car miles ahead of contemporary efforts by others, such as Austin and Ford, but the YA brakes were not known for their efficiency. It was only when the TD was developed on the Y's excellent thin-walled 14 SWG boxed-in chassis that all-new Girling twin-leading-shoe (TLS) front brakes arrived. According to MG literature these TLS brakes were fitted from YB No. 286, so from the first car at No. 251 YA parts were still used. YB rear brakes remained with a single leading shoe and one trailing shoe or the car would have become virtually brakeless in reverse. For the uninitiated, leading shoes are those that come on and are actually dragged on more in a self-servo action by the rotation of the brake drum, giving far better braking if travelling forwards. A leading shoe has its leading edge touch the drum first. A trailing shoe is one that the rotation of the brake drum tries to push away the shoe, hindering the brake's action (but driving backwards this trailing shoe becomes a leading shoe). Lo and behold, BMC reintroduced the SLS front brakes on the 1959 Mini to keep costs low. Those who drove these early Minis will remember those poor brakes. BMC were soon forced to fit TLS brakes, then discs, then servo-assisted discs.

So, the YB gained the later Girling twin-leading-shoe front brakes from the TD, though such a system requires two front brake cylinders to each side, as each shoe is individually operated. It has been known for amateur restorers to fit the brake back plates onto the wrong side of the car, continuing to assemble the brakes in such a fashion they have ended up with a full set of trailing shoes. As the car will have awful forward brakes the MOT examiner soon picks this error up. Not only did the YB braking system gain modern drum brake technology, the system itself was different from that fitted to the previous YA. The YB drums were also one-piece wheel bearing hub castings – the drums could not be removed separately as on the YA.

Well into YB production, at car No. 286 again, the rear axle was changed from the Morris banjo spiral-bevel type to the Nuffield split variety with hypoid gears. This was a much stronger, quieter and longer-lived axle than the pre-war Morris unit fitted to the YA. The YB's axle gained the one-piece, five-stud brake drums as well, fitting onto a locating tapered collar and splined drive shaft end with a very large nut. Hiding all this brake technology were 5.50 by 15-inch wheels – 1 inch smaller than those on the YA of 5.00 by 16 inches. To improve the looks of the model, YB rear wings were given a deeper skirt than the YA – the most obvious visual difference between the two versions. Deeper rear wings must have been a current styling fad, as the 803-cc Morris Minor S2 also lost its slimmer rear wings to deeper versions on the 948-cc Minor 1000 shortly after. Chromed steel hub caps on the YB were smaller and had an unpainted MG motif, cast in Mazak, in the centre. Later YA/YTs had the MG motif as well. YB hub caps are identical to those on the TD, TF, ZA, ZB, ZBF and Farina Magnettes, though after 1960 they are stainless-steel spun pressings. Hidden well from view was a more modern brake master-cylinder mounted aft of the pedal box. Not only the type of rear axle, but also rear axle ratios, differed between the YA and YB – the YA was 5.143:1 and the YB was 5.125:1. (The same axle and ratio used in the Wolseley 4/44 and Morris MO series. These cars only had standard BMC four stud wheel fixings, though.)

The spare wheel cover was deeper on the YB to take the larger section 5.50 tyre, but this is hard to see with the eye. Other supposed updates of the electrical system were fed in piecemeal. Current books say the YB had a later Lucas RB106 control box with a separate fuse box, though early YB owners such as myself will tell you these were not fitted for quite some months into production, at car No. 326 to be exact. It is a bit like saying the YB has the SC2 version of the XPAG engine when in fact a number of the last YA's had this engine with the integral oil filter cast onto the side of the oil pump.

I recently read that the YA did not handle as well as was expected. It roll-over-steered a little too readily and, considering it had a rear Panhard rod to control rear axle side movement, this surprised me. Anyway, MG decided the Panhard rod was expensive and not required, so it was deleted from the YB. At the same time MG modified the IFS geometry by lowering the bottom wishbone fulcrum point on the chassis cross member. You can see the welded-on beam the lower arm's now bolted to – between the arms and the cross member. This lowered the roll centre and to ensure the car sat better on corners, a front anti-roll bar was fitted. As the MGA and MGB use a virtually identical IFS system, it is again interesting to see how these sports cars' anti-roll bars link to the suspension when compared to the YB's arrangement. On the YB the link bolts to the upper flat face of the spring seat. This cracks after many years use, around the bolt heads. On the other cars the link bolts to holes drilled in the front wishbone arm – a much stronger position. It is nice to know that MGA lower arms, kingpins and seat pans fit a Y type (as do MGB items, especially the longer-lived MGB V8 inner rubber bushes). The MGB kingpins are very different, though look similar externally. Dampers were improved at the rear on the YB, though their basic lever-arm design was similar. The YB has heavy-duty rear dampers. Road tests spoke of the better twin-tone horns of the YB, but these were not fitted to production models until car No. 460. Headlamp shells were smaller on the YB to take the standard 7-inch Lucas pre-focus lamp unit, but again this was not easily seen by the eye.

So, it is hard to decide exactly where the YB began, what with late YAs getting the later engine and other parts taking ages to arrive. Or was it just a case of using up current production items and feeding in the new parts when old items ran out? MG must have taken the decision at a point in production to say, 'YBs Start Here.' It is a little worrying when you realise that the last YA was Y7285 and the first YB was YB0251, leaving Abingdon on 21 November 1951, when the only real difference between the two was the wheel size, anti-roll bar, lower bottom wishbone and rear-wing valance depth. The YA already had the SC2 XPAG engine and the other updated items would arrive some months later such as improved TLS brakes, a better rear axle on car No. 0286, control box on No. 0326, and finally twin-tone horns on car No. 460.

What would Trading Standards make of that today? The adverts had promised all the updates. Perhaps that is why the motoring press was reluctant in those days to feature updated cars.

8

MG's Advertising Booklet of 1947

Introduction

There is more than tradition behind the marque ⊛, and in presenting this entirely new conception of an ⊛ car, the outstanding characteristics of its predecessors have been faithfully maintained.

The "One and a Quarter" Litre ⊛ Saloon has been developed and produced in the "atmosphere" peculiar to the marque, but with a firm purpose in view.

That goal has been achieved by the provision of a car with the utmost luxury per horse power—a new standard perhaps—yet economical to acquire and own.

Maintaining the Breed

*T*he style, dignity and grace of this new Saloon are manifest to a casual observer. Its roominess, comfort, riding and equipment are impressive.

In road behaviour and performance, the "One and a Quarter" Saloon is really outstanding. Perfect traffic manners; an unusual capacity to cover long or short journeys at high averages; 🅜 acceleration and superb braking power, justify the slogan "Safety Fast!"

The 🅜 "One and a Quarter" Litre Saloon is proudly offered to discriminating motorists—built to the high 🅜 standard, ... it "Maintains the Breed".

*D*escribed by one expert as "a very capable and very obliging car" it can show a "clean pair of heels" should occasion demand; a delight to drive and handle in the densest traffic of a city, the "One and a Quarter" will take you out into the country with verve and zest —"Do you know England?".

Maintaining the Breed

Would you explore Scotland—Wales? Here is a most modern conception of a low powered economical car. A willing climber with superb braking power and comfort, this new ⊕ Saloon, lacking nothing of its antecedents'.qualities of materials and workmanship, provides the delights of Real Motoring.

Maintaining the Breed

1. Extremely rigid chassis employing fully boxed side members electrically welded throughout.

2. Fingerlight, positive, direct acting rack and pinion steering with adjustable wheel position.

3. Independent wishbone type coil spring front suspension.

4. Unusually long laminated rubber interleaved rear springs.

5. Lockheed hydraulic brakes operate on large area drums—a "Safety Fast!" feature.

6. Integral Jackall jacks operated from nearside of Engine.

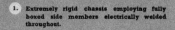

Details of the One and

The arrangement of the independent front wheel suspension is simple, sturdy, and mechanically highly efficient.

The control lever for the Jackall system is conveniently placed under the bonnet. Of easiest access, disturbing no passengers.

Page six

68

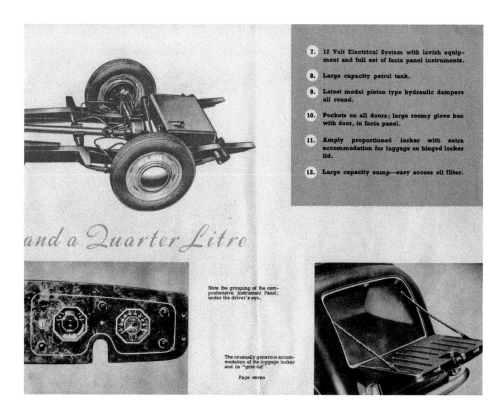

7. 12 Volt Electrical System with lavish equipment and full set of facia panel instruments.

8. Large capacity petrol tank.

9. Latest model piston type hydraulic dampers all round.

10. Pockets on all doors; large roomy glove box with door, in facia panel.

11. Amply proportioned locker with extra accommodation for luggage on hinged locker lid.

12. Large capacity sump—easy access oil filter.

and a Quarter Litre

Note the grouping of the comprehensive Instrument Panel; under the driver's eye.

The unusually generous accommodation of the luggage locker and its "grid-lid".

Page seven

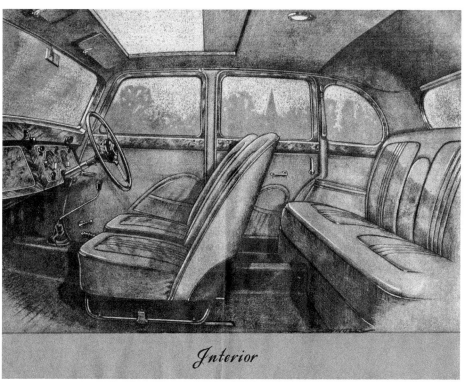

Interior

69

*J*llustrating unusual luxury and comfort in the interior — ample headroom and legroom.

All cabinet work is carried out in selected Walnut, including the garnish rails and window fillets. The glove box is of attractive dimensions, and is intended to be of useful service. Pockets in all doors, and ashtrays are provided.

Upholstered throughout in a new style in high grade leather of pleasing shades; cushions are panelled and piped. Both front seats are adjustable, and a folding arm-rest is provided in the rear squab. Assist Slings are also fitted for rear passengers.

Deep pile carpet covers the floor entirely, and a reinforcement mat is fitted for the driver's use.

Gear change and brake levers are so placed as to be instantly at hand—yet completely unobtrusive to the front passenger. Wide doors and a well-less floor give easy and dignified ingress or egress.

Page nine

70

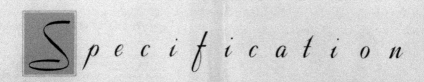

Specification

ENGINE: Cylinder Bore 66.5 mm. Stroke 90 mm. 1250 cc. R.A.C. rating 10.97 h.p. Counter-balanced crankshaft, three main bearings. Con. rods of H section steel, loose steel shell white metal bearings. Pistons of controlled expansion aluminium alloy. Overhead valves operated by push rods through rockers. 14 mm. plugs, Champion L/10 S. 12 volt coil ignition, automatic advance. Force feed lubrication, pressure oil filter, 100%, filtration. Aluminium alloy sump, capacity 1½ gallons (5 litres). Oil filler in accessible position on the valve cover. Camshaft drive Duplex roller chain with hydraulic tensioner. Carburettor Single S.U. semi-downdraught. Air cleaner. Radiator fan. Water circulated by pump; temperature thermostatically controlled. 12 volt sliding pinion type electric starter, with control switch on instrument panel.

TRANSMISSION: Borg and Beck dry clutch. Four speed gearbox, Second, Third, and Top synchromesh. Gear ratios: Top—5.143 to 1; Third—7.121 to 1; Second—10.646 to 1; First—18.0 to 1; Reverse—18.0 to 1. Gear change lever is centrally situated with reverse gear stop. Propeller shaft Hardy Spicer needle bearing, dynamically balanced. Rear axle, three-quarter floating, spiral bevel drive. Ratio: 5.143 to 1.

FUEL: 8-gallon (36-litres) tank at rear. Quick filler with snap type cap. S.U. petrol pump. Flexible piping to carburettor.

CHASSIS: Track Front 3' 11¼' (1 m. 475); Rear 4' 2' (1 m. 270); Wheelbase 8' 3' (2 m. 538); Clearance 6" (0 m. 150) at lowest point. Construction is of sturdy "boxed" type side members, underslung at the rear, with robust tubular cross members; electrically welded throughout and employing the most modern engineering developments.

SUSPENSION: In front, the latest development of MG wishbone type, independently sprung wheels employing coil springs and rubber bushed inner mountings. At rear, long flexible laminated springs rubber interleaved, mounted in rubber bushes, with which is incorporated an additional refinement by the provision of a rubber mounted lateral control link to stabilise rear axle movement. Luvax Girling piston type hydraulic dampers complete a sound, comfortable suspension. Chassis lubrication by grease gun nipples at necessary points.

ELECTRICAL EQUIPMENT: Electrical wiring is single pole and the circuit has two fuses for simplicity. 12 volt coil and automatically controlled distributor. Dynamo, belt driven from crankshaft, operates in conjunction with a compensating voltage control unit. Battery is automatically charged at correct rate required by load and state of charge. Lucas high frequency horn. Twin screen wipers with remote driving motor. Traffic indicators, electrically controlled in centre of steering wheel, having delayed action return switch.

LIGHTING: Lighting switches on instrument panel. Two C.P. Headlamps, dip-switch, operated by foot control. Two wing lamps. Twin tail lamps. "Stop" light, automatically controlled by brake pedal. Fog lamp with separate control switch. Reversing light, automatically controlled by engagement of reverse gear. Roof light, with control switch over driving seat.

BRAKES: Highly efficient Lockheed hydraulic brakes. Large area drums, 9' diameter, (0 m. 230), Ferodo linings. Pedal operates on all four wheels. Adjustments at each brake drum. Independent central hand brake, cable operated on rear wheels only, with conveniently placed adjusting nuts at base of hand brake lever.

WHEELS: Disc type, with large chromium plated centres. Size 3.00' × 16'. Tyres by Dunlop, size 5.25' × 16' E.L.P.

JACKING SYSTEM: Jackall built-in, with control on left hand side under bonnet. Quick, convenient, and clean.

STEERING: Direct acting, rack and pinion type, light and positive. Steering column is adjustable for 3' (0 m. 80) movement. 16½' (0 m. 420) diameter spring spoked wheel, with comfortably shaped rim. Turning circle, R.H., 35' 5' (10 m. 795), L.H., 34' 10' (10 m. 617) radius.

INSTRUMENTS: Ammeter, oil pressure and petrol gauges. Speedometer and electric clock. Speedometer registers M.P.H., trip mileage, and total mileage covered by car. Instrument panel has diffused lighting for night driving.

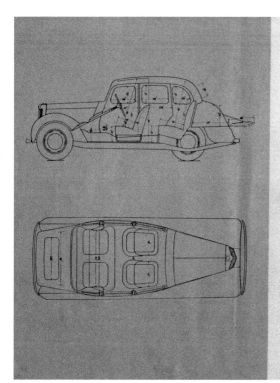

Specification (cont.)

COACHWORK: Is on the luxury level. All cabinet work including the facia board, instrument panel, garnish rails, and the window fillets, is carried out in walnut.

Comfort, roominess, and luxury have been achieved throughout. There is plenty of headroom, and the well designed windows give an unimpeded view to driver and passengers.

Trimmed and upholstered throughout in high grade leather of pleasing neutral tint in an exclusive style.

The driving seat has a wide range of adjustment, front passenger seat is also adjustable. Rear seat has a centre arm rest, and assist pulls at either side.

Pile carpet back and front with a rubber reinforcement mat on driver's floor. Sun visors are supplied for both driver and front seat passenger. The windscreen is opening-adjustable type with central easy-winding control, providing means of ventilation and avoidance of "Misting". Winding windows to all four doors. Triplex toughened glass throughout. The "flush-fitting" sliding panel in the roof has been skilfully designed to ensure that rear passengers are not subject to draught. Rear blind controlled by driver.

Roof light with switch in roof above driver's head.

A spacious glove-box is fitted opposite the front passenger seat, well lined, with drop front. Ashtrays are provided.

Excellent accommodation is arranged for luggage in the rear compartment. The lid opens downwards to act as an additional luggage carrier when required.

The spare wheel and tool kit compartment are in a separate locker at the rear of the car, and are completely accessible with a full load of luggage.

A comprehensive set of tools is provided.

DIMENSIONS

Overall length	.. ..	161"	4 m. 89
Overall height	.. ..	58'	1 m. 473
Overall width	.. ..	59'	1 m. 499
Width of rear seats, at elbow	.. ..	45½'	1 m. 156
Width of rear seats, at seat	.. ..	40'	1 m. 16
Height floor to roof, at rear seats	..	44'	1 m. 118
Height floor to top of seat cushion, rear	..	12'	0 m. 305
Front seat back from foot ramp. 42½' min.		47½' max.	1 m. 207
Width of each front seat	..	19'	0 m. 483
Length of each front seat	.. ..	18'	0 m. 457
Width at front seats, pillar to pillar	..	45'	1 m. 143
Total adjustment on Driver's seat, plus steering column		8'	0 m. 203
Height of front seats	.. .. ..	10'	0 m. 254
Top of front seat cushion to bottom of steering wheel	.. .. ..	6½'	0 m. 165

NUFFIELD EXPORTS LTD

VISCOUNT NUFFIELD, G.B.E., *Chairman*   Telegrams and Cables · MORRIS, OXFORD   SIR MILES THOMAS, D.F.C., *Vice-Chairman*
Telephone · OXFORD 77731   Telex · OXFORD TELEX 7148
COWLEY   **OXFORD**   **ENGLAND**

Safety **MG** fast!

Designed and printed by
The Nuffield Press Ltd., Oxford, England,
in collaboration with
Seward, Baker & Co. Ltd.

9

Ys in the Twenty-first Century

If you have never owned and run an elderly classic car, it will come as a bit of a shock to find out just how much servicing an old car requires. Whereas your twenty-first-century SUV will go 12,000 miles between servicing and most of its components are either sealed or lubricated for life, the MG Y Type you have just bought needs a great deal more TLC. If you are not of a mechanical mind you are going to need to find a sympathetic garage that knows about old cars. Your average service station and MOT testing station may not even own a grease gun, let alone an oil gun. The average hourly labour charge at a garage for classic cars is around £60 (2020). Servicing a Y Type there would take around three hours, providing they have things like grease guns. Oil, filter, plugs, condenser and points would cost around £80. If you did it yourself you can buy the parts online from Moss or Brown and Gammons for around £50, getting the oil from your local motor factors. You need to check your cylinder head's use of either short-reach or long-reach plugs. See the casting number section in Chapter 5.

The Y Type has a multitude of grease nipples and one oil nipple, which require regular attention. For instance, the kingpins need grease every 500 miles, and steering joints and universal joints every 1,000 miles. The engine oil needs changing every 3,000 miles, and gearbox and rear axle oil every 6,000 miles. You will need a handbook if you are to DIY servicing. The steering rack is the one oil nipple that requires very smelly hypoid gear oil – same as the rear axle. It can be very satisfying to service your own car, setting ignition points, changing plugs, setting tappets and so on. You can cheat these days by fitting electronic ignition and if your Y does not already have flashing indicators, there are good LED sets on the market. Many Y owners now fit LED rear lights and headlamp bulbs, as it gives the dynamo a much easier life. Then there is the way that dynamo (and water pump) are driven – by a fan belt. It is best to carry a spare as they break at the most inopportune moments. The most awkward bits to DIY grease are the pedal box and propeller shaft joints. Always use axle stands when going under the car; do not trust the jack-all system on its own. Using a trolley jack, only jack on the chassis, never the body, and watch out for garage mechanics here used to monocoque cars.

Semaphore trafficators are not seen or looked for by today's drivers. LED flashing indicator kits are available.

LED headlamp and rear light/brake lights are available and take less power than the old tungsten filament bulbs.

While back in 1947 the little MG was a front-line performer, the Y is now a very pedestrian car on the road – its performance is feeble compared to today's cars, so you need to drive it to cope. You cannot cruise it at 70 mph on a motorway as it may not go that fast as well as risking blowing up the engine. 45–50 mph is a fast cruising speed for a 1930s car; to get a better mpg 35–40 mph is more reasonable. The gear change is slow: you need to move the lever out of one gear, wait a fraction of a second, then select the next gear. The synchromesh cones are small, and you cannot whisk through the gears as on a modern car. Braking will be a revelation to you. They are drum brakes and your foot is the power assistance. You need to apply them using quite some force compared to your modern servo-assisted, ventilated, disc-braked pocket rocket. You will soon find they are pretty good, but you need to push that pedal hard. Likewise, the steering is not light, though it is very accurate. With cross-ply tyres, slow manoeuvring for parking will test your biceps; with radial-ply tyres you will have to move the car a bit to get that steering wheel to turn due to the much-improved grip. That is why the steering wheel is of a big diameter – to give you the required leverage.

Filling up at the petrol station is not easy either, unlike your modern car you cannot rely on the tank's back pressure to switch off the delivery pump nozzle. The filler pipe is too big, so no back pressure is generated for the delivery nozzle to sense. You need to read the fuel gauge contents to know roughly how much to put in to not get a blow back and petrol-soaked shoes. The tank takes 8 gallons. If your engine has not had hardened-steel exhaust valve seats fitted to cope with lead-free petrol, you will also need to put an additive

Oil, water and tyres pressures are a weekly task on old cars.

in every time you fill up to protect those soft cast-iron valve seats from burning away. The Y was built when petrol had tetraethyllead (TEL) in it to stop the engine pinking (pre-ignition) and enabled higher compression ratios. It also acted as a lubricant for the exhaust valve seat by depositing a micro-thin layer of lead in the exhaust valve's seat, greatly assisting the heat transfer from the valve to the cylinder head. This advantage meant there was no need for the manufacturer to shrink in or cast in a hardened steel exhaust-valve seats into the head. They could use the cheap cast iron the head was made of directly, which saved money. But when TEL was removed from petrol cast-iron valve seats began to burn away at an alarming rate, ruining older engines. Either an additive is now required or hardened steel valve seats fitting. Also, you will need to check that the brass float in the carburettor float chamber has been swapped for a 'stay-up' plastic float from Burlen. Ethanol dissolves the tin-based solder that holds the two halves of the brass float together and the float fills with fuel. This will make the car undriveable. Rubber and plastic fuel pipes will also need changing for ethanol-resistant material. Currently ethanol is 5 % of fuel, but it is soon to be 11 %. Firms like Burlen sell the required ethanol-resistant items for your fuel system. If your fuel gauge stops working, suspect one of two things: either the wire contact on the contents float just behind the offside rear wheel has corroded and is no longer making contact, or the ethanol in the petrol has eaten away the tin on the solder inside the tank on the rheostat section of the contents float.

Hopefully the car you have taken a shine to has been rewired with modern plastic-insulated cables. The original cotton-covered rubber wires will by now be lethal,

Greasing the steering, suspension, cables and water pump are another regular servicing requirement.

though some plastic wire can be bought with cotton covering to look like the older wiring for originality. An insurance company will want to know of the age of the wiring for Agreed Value purposes. Agreed Value Insurance is different to the normal fully comp and TPFT. It actually insures the car for a prearranged, agreed value. For this you have to supply proof of the car's condition and its value – usually a set of photos if your valuation is of the average but possibly also an engineer's report if yours is concours.

Checking what you are looking at is important, though few Y Types are fakes these days. In the past it has been known for a Y chassis to find its way underneath a T Type body, as T Types are about 30 % more valuable and a TF 50 %; even a YT will be almost double a YA's selling price. A YA's chassis number will actually start with just a Y as there was no other version then. They begin at Y0251 and end at Y7285. The YT's chassis number are in among the YA's, but have YT as the prefix. The first was YT1922, so YT numbers do not have their own system as the car uses a YA chassis. The YB starts at YB0251 and ends at YB1551. Y production ran from March 1947 to August 1953. The colour scheme of your Y would originally have either been a single tone all over, or two-tone with the body one colour and the wings and running boards another. Today you will find non-standard, two-tone finishes where the body swage line has been used to split them. Often a lighter colour is used and makes the car look longer and even lower.

It is well worth warning others if you use a motorway or fast dual-carriageway.

Do not get caught buying the wrong starter motor. Either a nine- or ten-tooth bendix is fitted, so check first.

Each week you need to check the oil and water level (coolant) in the engine. That XPAG unit was never very oil-tight, even when new; its asbestos-string front crankshaft seal and the reverse-scroll rear crankshaft sealing are the best 1938 could provide. Right up until the 1960s UK cars used similar engine sealing, and nearly all rear-wheel-drive (RWD) cars with front engines of that era drip oil from the little hole under the clutch bell housing. On many Y Types now you will find a little drip tray fitted to catch this small leak, so as to not upset those they visit with posh, clean, stone driveways. Checking water and oil weekly (and more often if doing high mileages each day) will come as a bit of a shock to the younger owner used to their 12,000 miles between servicing a modern car. The radiator cap is a real one and it gets hot. Check its level once a week and top up with the correct mixture of water and antifreeze to the bottom of the filler. Do not fill to the top as the water will expand once heated by the engine and flow out of the overflow pipe and out under the car. You will then think you have a big leak or, if you miss the pool underneath, you will think it is using a lot as you need to keep topping up a lot. You will need to top the radiator up often as the cooling system is of the 1930s – the era of the car. It is not pressurised as in a modern car. As the system is working at ambient air pressure and is not sealed, the water will evaporate. Carry a spare container of coolant in the spare wheel compartment for long trips.

Two areas that will most certainly be unfamiliar are the opening windscreen and steel sliding sunroof. Both are identical to the donor, the Morris Eight Series E, and were also

Some have fitted 1,800-cc MGB engines that make the Y really fly, but beware of losing the VHI entitlement.

used on the Wolseley Eight. The windscreen can be opened by the little winding handle on the top of the dash. New seals are available and fiddly to fit, and do not quite follow the original section. Be prepared to get the odd leak in really heavy rain – have a sponge and chamois leather handy. As the windscreen opens the law says the car is not required to have windscreen washers, but it must be able to open and not be sealed up. The other trap for the unwary is the sunroof. Its runners may well require greasing if unused for some time. There are drain tubes running from each corner of the sunroof rails. These can become blocked with leaf mould if not cleaned out regularly – you will find this out when letting out the clutch to move off and a waterfall cascades onto your and the passenger's laps. The rubber pipes require the headlining to be removed and the steel pipe part on the rails is often very corroded. By far the worst bit is getting the old ones out of and the new ones into the insides of the windscreen pillars – the front drainpipes run down these.

The kingpins can be bent if you kerb the car very hard or hit a very deep pothole. It is advisable to steer clear on potholes unless you want an expensive front suspension rebuild. Luckily, the kingpins are identical to those of the MGA sports car so still available. There is no provision for the fitting of seat belts, nor is the body stressed for fitting them. If you want them you will need to find a specialist who can modify the chassis to take them. When the car was used in rallies full harnesses were used and this makes the rear seats unusable. When the car was first tested by the *Motor* and *Autocar*, they said the steering

MGCC annual Silverstone event attracts many MGs.

was light. Compared to 1950s cars, it was; today it seems heavy as most cars now have power-assisted steering, even the small ones. With its tiny 30 bhp per litre in today's traffic the acceleration is very pedestrian indeed and allowance must be made for this by other motorists, especially exiting roundabouts. They will accelerate and suddenly find they are nearly ramming into the rear of an old car. They will sound their horn at you telling you to speed up, not thinking of the 150 bhp in their light alloy and plastic box.

Should you want to MOT your car, even though it is currently exempt in the UK, you will have to convince the tester that the body number plate they are studying is not the chassis number. Unfortunately, the body number is easy to see on the nearside dash/firewall. The correct chassis number is on the brass plate on the side of the battery box. The body number was given by the Nuffield company, who built it within their own system. The chassis number was given by the MG Car Company Ltd.

The windscreen wipers are another oddity to modern drivers. While they are driven by an electric motor on the offside of the dash under the bonnet by a cable, they are operated by the big Bakelite knobs on the cant rail under the windscreen. That on the driver's side can be used by hand for a one-wipe action by pressing and holding it in all the time, and then by the electric motor if the knob is released as it engages with the sprocket driven by that motor's cable. The ignition needs to be switched on and the wiper knob twisted until the engagement is felt. To get the passenger side one to follow again their knob needs depressing and the wiper bought up onto the screen where the driving cable will pick it up.

2015 Y Register Spring Run, an annual event.

To park either blade requires depressing the knob and turning the blade until it is off the windscreen and parked on the top of the dash. Beware the passenger who tries to wipe their side as you engage the motor (on a switch hidden under the cant rail and automatic) and your wiper strikes theirs. This will force the wiper's arm to twist on its mounting collett on the little sprocket driven by that cable. The wiper will then not be central, and on its return wipe it will carry on down onto the paintwork of the dash under the windscreen and plough a groove in it. You have been warned; it's best to ban any passengers from touching that knob.

As the car never had a temperature gauge, many fit a 1930s calorimeter to the radiator cap with its foot down in the water. While enthusiasts will say it's not for a post-war car, others will not know. At least you will be able to see if the engine is getting hot – by a broken fan belt, for instance. A fault with this type of gauge is when the water level gets below the foot, as it just then measures the air temperature, so if you look as if you are running cool, check the coolant's level often. Park the blades on the dash top because if you open the windscreen you are likely to engage that motor and cause more damage. They are not left on the screen as on modern cars.

If you have to use a motorway, try to do so on a quiet period, although the M25 is often only doing about 35–40 mph when I go to the annual Brooklands MG Day. Keep your eyes on that rearview mirror and be prepared to take to the hard shoulder when it's obvious the vehicle coming up behind you is going too fast. Fit wing mirrors.

A YA with MGB running gear including chromed spoke wheels.

Disc brake kits are available, at a price.

Note that there are two different lengths of engine dipstick. It was lengthened so it could be reached when a LHD steering column was fitted from engine number SC2/13404. Fitting the earlier, short dipstick means you will overfill the sump.

The rear leaf springs, if original, may have settled and the clips worn slots into the top leaf. This slot creates an area of stress and the leaf can break. If a top leaf breaks the rear axle will move about and you will require a recovery lorry. The Luvax-Girling lever-arm dampers will eventually leak, but NTG of Ipswich can do a reconditioned-exchange service.

Today it is well worth fitting LED sidelights, headlights, indicators and brake lights. They take a lot less power than the old tungsten filament bulbs, giving the dynamo an easier life. The gauges need brighter bulbs as well and they are fiddly to get to. The old semaphore trafficators can be fitted with flashing festoon bulbs and so become a repeater; on their own they simply are not seen by the modern road user. Electronic ignition is another good idea, but for all these electrical items you need to know your car's polarity, positive or negative earth? If you need to change it to suit LEDs, your ammeter will read backwards and your ignition coil will need its wires switching over.

As the MGA and MGB use a similar kingpin, it is possible to fit disc brakes to a Y – NTG sell a kit just for this modification. But you will need to fit an extra master cylinder reservoir and a servo because the pistons in a disc brake move more fluid as the pads wear and discs require very high pressure. A servo does not improve drum brakes, it only makes them easier to apply.

The fuel filler cap on the Y is a big opening, unlike the tiny petrol car tank filler's today. So, it is only too easy to shove a diesel nozzle into it and fill up. As I was once told, there are those who have done it and those who eventually will.

The speedometers of the type and age fitted to Y Types is not that accurate. The regulations back then said they only need to be with plus or minus 5 %. Also, in 1954, the year after the model ended production, a law was passed that insisted all road vehicles have rear reflectors fitted. Check your car has them as they are not moulded into the rear light lenses. It was one of the very rare retrospective rules. Another oddity you will soon discover is that many council car park ANPR cameras cannot rear your old pre-1972 black-and-white number plates.

Security

This is not a car to leave out on the public road or in a car park overnight. The bonnet cannot be locked, it has no steering lock and is not alarmed. The door locks are easy to open. So, you will need to improve its security, if for no other reason than to please your insurers. Simplest device is a bit of steel tube – flattened one end and drilled for a padlock. Measure it up to fit over the handbrake lever fully 'on' and for the hole to line up with the gear lever in first or third. Padlock the lever to the tube. Also fit a battery-isolating switch to the starter solenoid, which can double up as a power-off switch when the car is in the garage and as an anti-theft device when outside. A hidden switch to cut off the SU fuel pump and/or ignition coil will help, though a thief may well 'hot-wire' the system. Finally have your car SelectaDNA fitted. Buy a tracker if your Y is really valuable.

10

Corrosion and Restoration

The majority of Y Types on the classic car market will have been restored by now as the Morris Eight Series E body tub is made of mild steel and was in no way protected against rust, especially inside box sections. The chassis is very long lived and only seems to rust at the bottom of the under-slung section under the rear axle. However, the body is of its era and the wings, where they bolt to the body, all around the rear spare wheel compartment, the C posts and inner wings, all corrode. Luckily, NTG of Ipswich do many repair panels for these areas, so your restorer can at least rebuild the car. Restoring a Y Type fully will

Mild steel reverting to ferrous-oxide having been stored under tarpaulins for years on damp soil. (Alan Chick)

cost far in excess of its market value. I have included some of the photos of my own 1952 YB that had major surgery at Brown & Gammons of Baldock in 2009. Body parts for Y Types are very, very scarce. Restoring, painting and trimming a Y Type is eye-wateringly expensive.

Beg, steal or borrow a copy of David Lawrence's book *Let There Be Ys* (now available from Paul Barrow on a CD, International Y Register) as this goes through the whole car bit by bit in great detail. It is invaluable for anyone about to restore a Y Type.

The XPAG engine has excellent spares back up as it is used in all those MG sports cars. While MG only recommended reboring to 0.040 in, the MG Octagon Car Club will sell you pistons for a rebore to 0.060 in. Most cylinder blocks can take this bigger boring, but be aware that internal corrosion over the vast number of years your block has existed may mean the boring might break through into the water jacket. Do not panic as the block has to then be re-linered back to its standard size. None of this is cheap. Photos of my block being bored by Headline of Park Farm, Wavendon, Milton Keynes, are shown.

Providing the gearbox does not have any broken teeth on its gears, especially the first on the layshaft, fitting new bearings and gasket (you will need to make your own gaskets) is not that expensive. Note the gearbox comes out of the car via the front seats, which need removing, as do the wooden floorboards and the gearbox cover.

Rotten sills being cut out. The body is left on its chassis to maintain rigidity. (B&G)

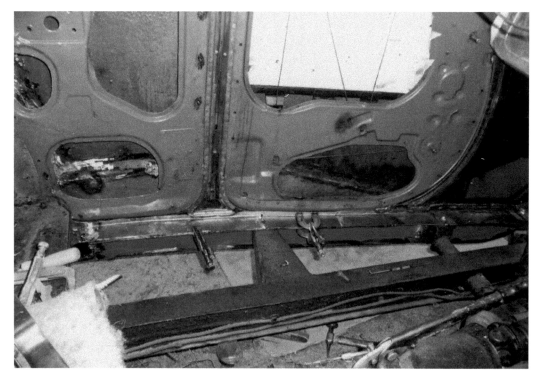

New sills being welded in, supplied by NTG. (B&G)

Chrome work is available new from NTG, but at a cost. The original Y Type bumpers are no longer available, but those meant for the TD Midget sports car will fit if you also buy the correct bumper irons (the support behind the bumper blade). YAs had no overriders; the YT had very slim ones of its own (now often fitted to YAs); and those on the YB are those meant for the TD and Wolseley 4/44.

On a windy day you might find yourself distracted by a dull rattle above your head. It might take some time to pinpoint it, but eventually you will notice the sunroof moving up and down very slightly in the gusts of the wind. The felt pads on the roof's runners have worn or become hardened. The screw that fixes the runners to the roof are hidden under the roof lining and are adjustable. Gluing new felt to them is easy: a bit of grease on the steel runners in the roof and a few days adjusting them till you get it just right will do.

Rear door windows might one day just drop into the door's insides. The winding frame on the window bottom has corroded away. New runners can be had from the MG Oct CC. The front door windows have a cable mechanism for winding them up and down. This wears out and the window jams. A rear brake inner bicycle cable will suffice from a cycle shop. The fluffy trim sections around all the door windows can be had from NTG of Ipswich.

Of all the jobs on a Y Type, renewing the headlining is the most difficult, I found. It's all in little bits pinned with tacks to wood or rolled up paper pressed into a channel. The bits of wood will have rotted away long ago so you have to use them as templates to make

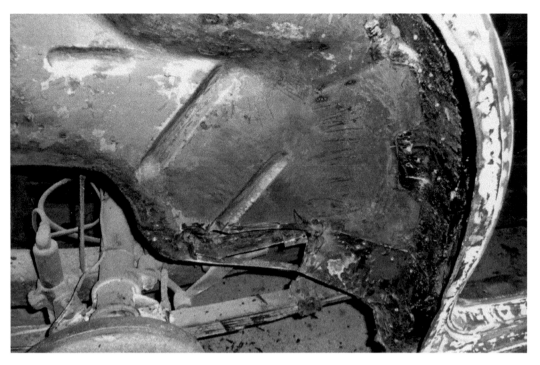

Bodged inner off-side wheel arch, a mass of odd bits of steel pop-rivetted on. (B&G)

New metal welded in. (B&G)

2018 was not a good year, but being a member of a club meant nearly all the bits required to fix this were soon found. Brown & Gammons did the work.

Dick Jacobs famously racing a YB here seen at Silverstone. The car is now in the Silverstone Museum.

new bits. NTG sell a kit for the job, but your knees will complain very quickly inside that small, low cab.

The tyres for the Y can be had from people like Vintage Tyres of the National Motor Museum, Beaulieu. Carburettor and fuel pump parts can be had from Burlen Fuel Services of Spitfire House, Salisbury. The MG Octagon Car Club and Moss stock a great many mechanical parts for your Y. You do need to remember that the YA and YT use mostly TB Midget parts, the YB uses MG TD/TF Midget parts. The specialists in those odd components for the Y Type are NTG of Ipswich, you can even get a full set of door cards, headlining kit and leather seat covers to fit your frames.

There is a full engine and gearbox rebuild on both the Y websites. Not a job for the faint hearted.

Today few have the skills required to carry out a full restoration. This means the use of specialist garages and it's very important to support such people, as if they disappear there is no one to supply the market and the car becomes doomed. The major cost in farming out any restoration is the labour charges per hour. No Y Type is going to be worth what it will cost to do a full restoration yet. Many of my age group did engineering apprenticeships and are capable of servicing and maintaining the car, but if you do not have this then the

Andrew Moreland racing his YT. (Andrew Moreland)

Water seems to play a lot in Y Register runs.

cost of very regular servicing needs to be factored in to the car's running costs. Even once restored the car will not stay pristine for very long, requiring the odd touch-up. It is best to learn how and where to grease the car yourself and buy a good quality grease gun. Use barrier cream on your hands if you do.

Buying a Y Type today requires great caution. Like most things made of untreated mild steel, they rot away very quickly. It would be best to read up as much as possible on the car, and look on the website pages and Facebook pages recommended in this book for the queries people ask about to keep their cars running and for classic car shows being attended (MG Day at Brooklands is a good bet here as well as the MGCC Silverstone event). Talk to the owners about their cars and what to look for. Beware cars for sale that keep appearing unsold: they are probably way overpriced or very tatty. Buy the best one you can afford; restoring a Y Type fully can cost a fortune. The most expensive and rarest is the YT Tourer, many being reimported to the UK. The Y Type is also quite a rare model, many being broken up in the 1960s to 1970s for spares for the T Type Midgets. Become familiar with the no Road Tax payment required and no need for an MOT. Here the car must, by law, still obey all the requirements of an MOT. Y Types qualify as a Vehicle of Historic Interest (VHI) for DVLA. But beware modifying the car as such thing may affect its VHI status – DVLA issue guidance on this aspect. If your Y Type is removed from its VHI status it must have an annual MOT and may be difficult to insure.

11

Suppliers, Clubs and the End of the Y Type

Spares Suppliers

NTG of Ipswich, mgbits.com
Moss, moss-europe.co.uk
Brown & Gammons, ukmgparts.com
MG Octagon Car Club, mgoctagoncarclub.wordpress.com
Vintage Tyres, National Motor Museum, vintagetyres.com
Burlen Fuel Systems, burlen.co.uk

There are many others but not all deal with Y Types. See the adverts in the club magazines.

Clubs

MG Octagon Car Club, mgoctagoncarclub.wordpress.com
MG Car Club, mgcc.co.uk
MG Owner's Club, mgownersclub.co.uk

Belonging to a club is vital. In 2018, my own 1952 YB was involved in an accident that wrote off a front wing and most of the front suspension. I required a wing, a steering rack, a damper, a wheel and kingpins with suspension arms. I put out a wanted list on the MGCC Y Register Facebook page and by that evening had all I needed promised me. Without those contacts I would have been stumped and in serious trouble getting it repaired. I had agreed-value insurance and made the insurance company agree for Brown & Gammons of Baldock to carry out the repairs. They know old MGs very well and they supplied all the suspension parts, which are of course the same as the MGA. They had carried out the full body restoration and respray of the car in 2009.

The End of the Y Type

The last YB left Abingdon in August 1953 and production was down to a trickle. Some sat in showrooms until 1954 before they were sold, now looking distinctly old fashioned. By now the Nuffield empire had been taken over by Austin and had become the British Motor Corporation, BMC. The Y was replaced by the ZA Magnette, which was originally to use the twin-carburettor 1466 XPEG engine, but as BMC had taken over by then it used virtually all Austin A50 mechanics, though did have its own suspension and brakes with the Y's steering rack. The car that really followed the Y Type was the Wolseley 4/44. It was a chassisless monocoque very closely following the ZA, but came out in 1952 – a year before the MG. It uses all the Y Types' Nuffield running gear including the SC/2 engine, the rear axle, the gearbox modified to a column change system and brakes. The difference is the wheels, though looking identical to the YB they only have the four-stud BMC centres (YB has five). A 4/44 engine will drop into a YA, YT, YB, TB, TC, TD and TF only requiring a sump and manifold change. While the Y Type just made 8,336, the 4/44 rocketed past the 34,000 mark. It was, after all, a very up-to-date styled, streamlined, well-appointed car.

The 1952–56 Wolseley 4/44 uses the YB's SC/2 XPAG engine, but now called XPAW (W for Wolseley).

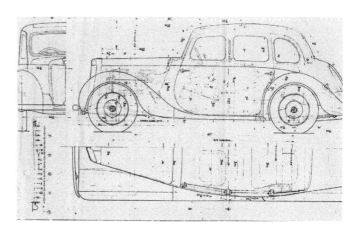

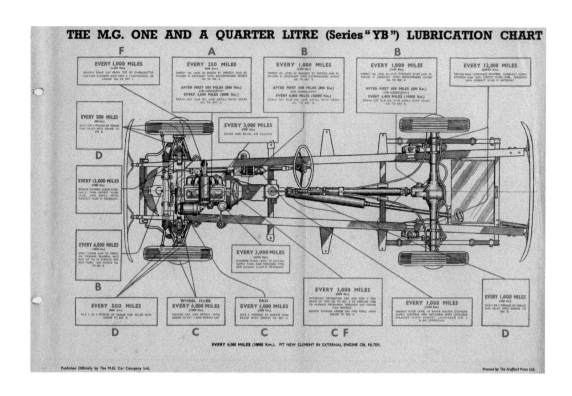

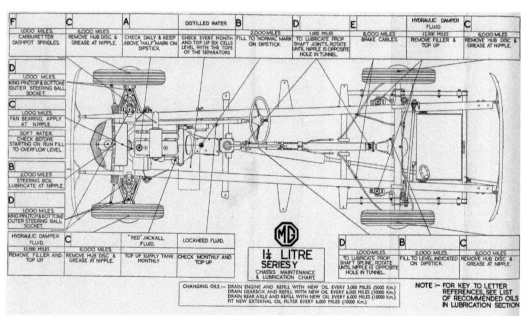

Bibliography

Books

Allison, Mike, *The Magic of the Marque* (Dalton Watson: 1989)

Cairns, Neil, *MG Engines 1935–1991* (available on the below websites under Technical Information)

Clausager, Anders Ditlev, *MG Saloon Cars 1920–70* (Bay View Books Ltd: 1998)

Knowles, David, *MG The Untold Story* (Motorbooks Intl: 1997)

Lawrence, David R., *Let There Be Ys* (ISBN 0-620-21832-0)

Lawson, John, *Y Type Saloons and Tourers* (Motor Racing Publications Ltd: 1988)

MG Y Types & Magnette ZA/ZB (Brooklands Books: 2009)

Websites

mgccyregister.co.uk

mg-cars.org.uk/imgytr

Both websites have for sale and wants pages.

Facebook

MGCarClub Y Register

MG Octagon Car Club

International Y Type Social Group

438 LRM